Christmas Doodle

by Lovink

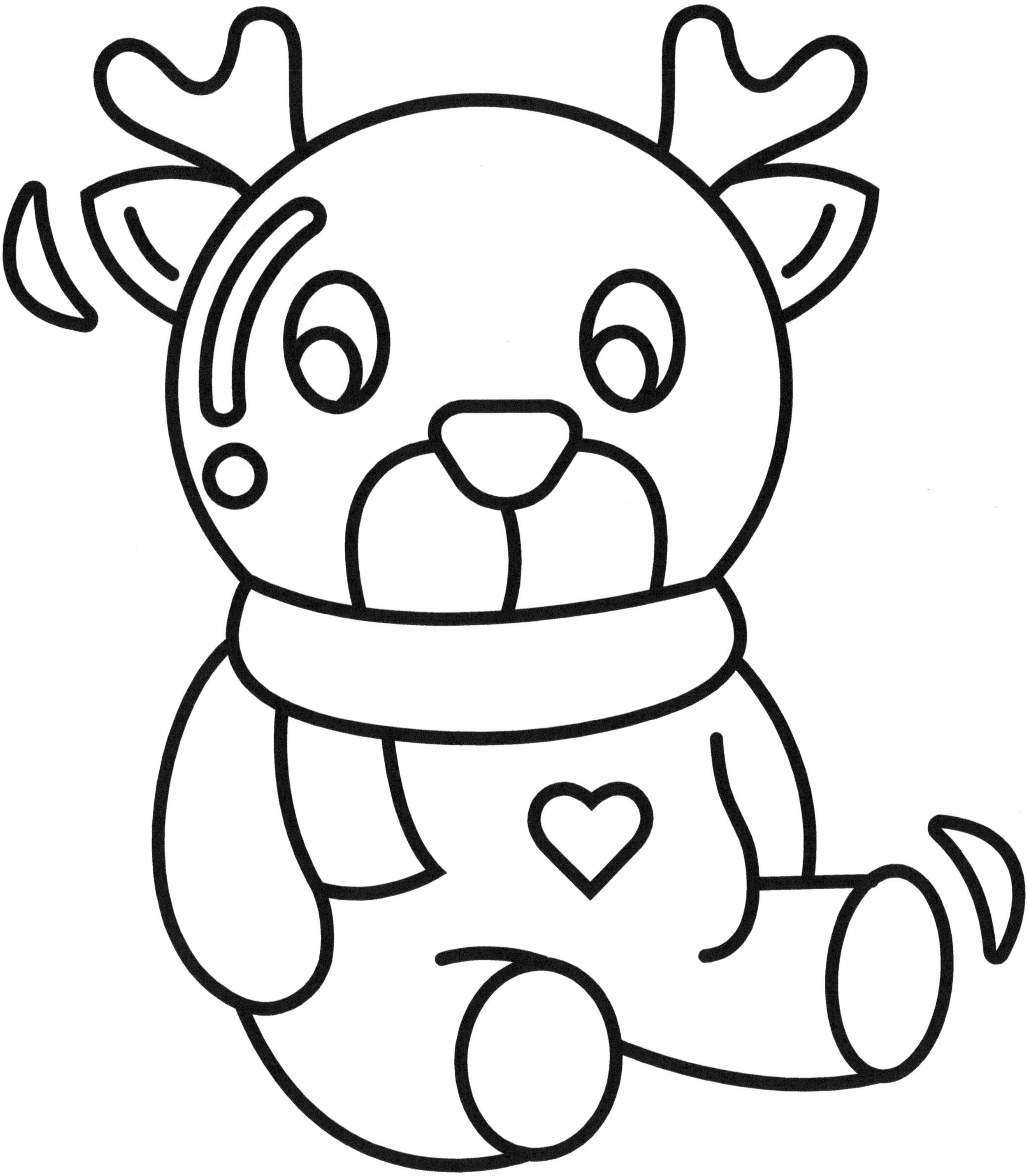

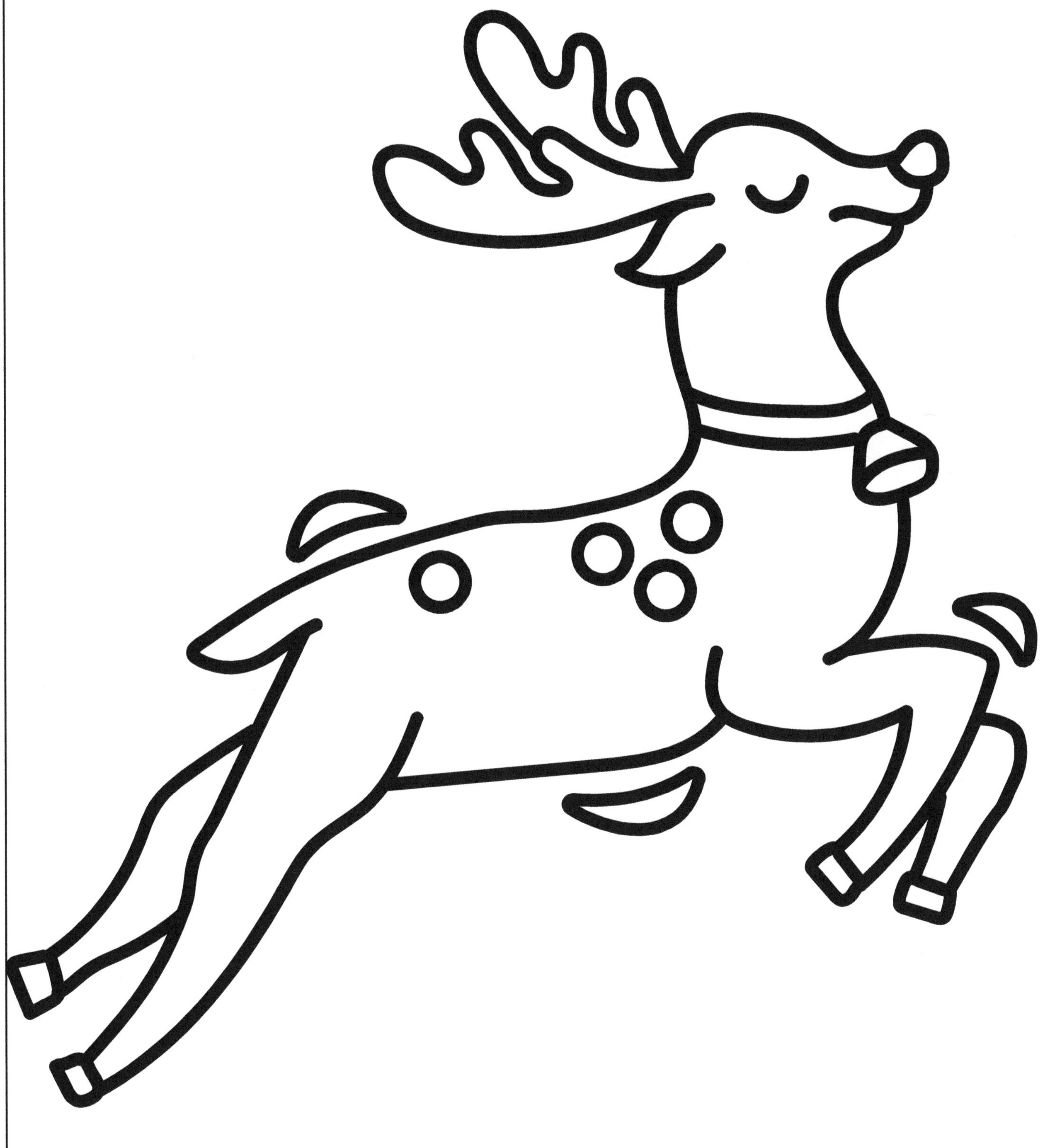

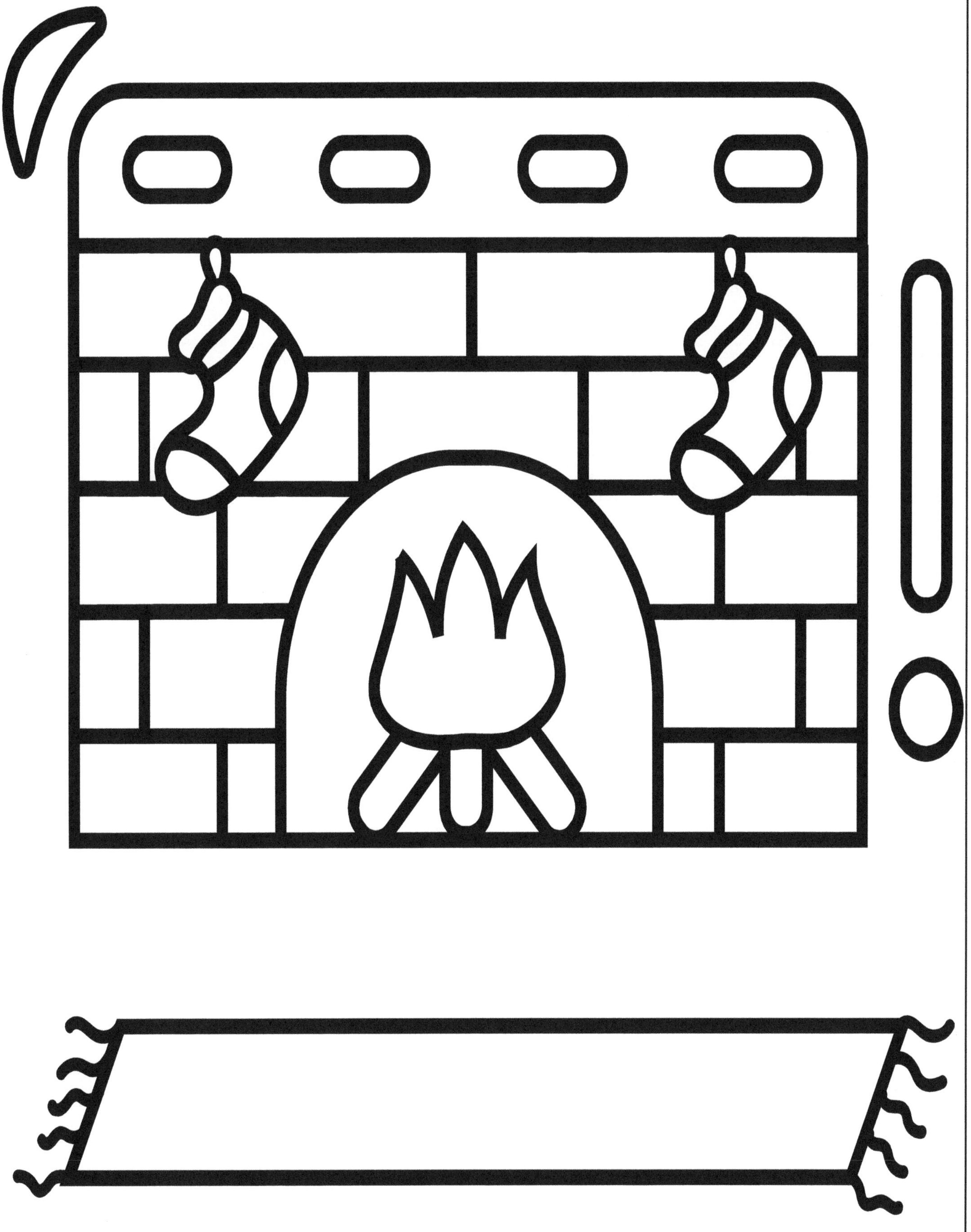

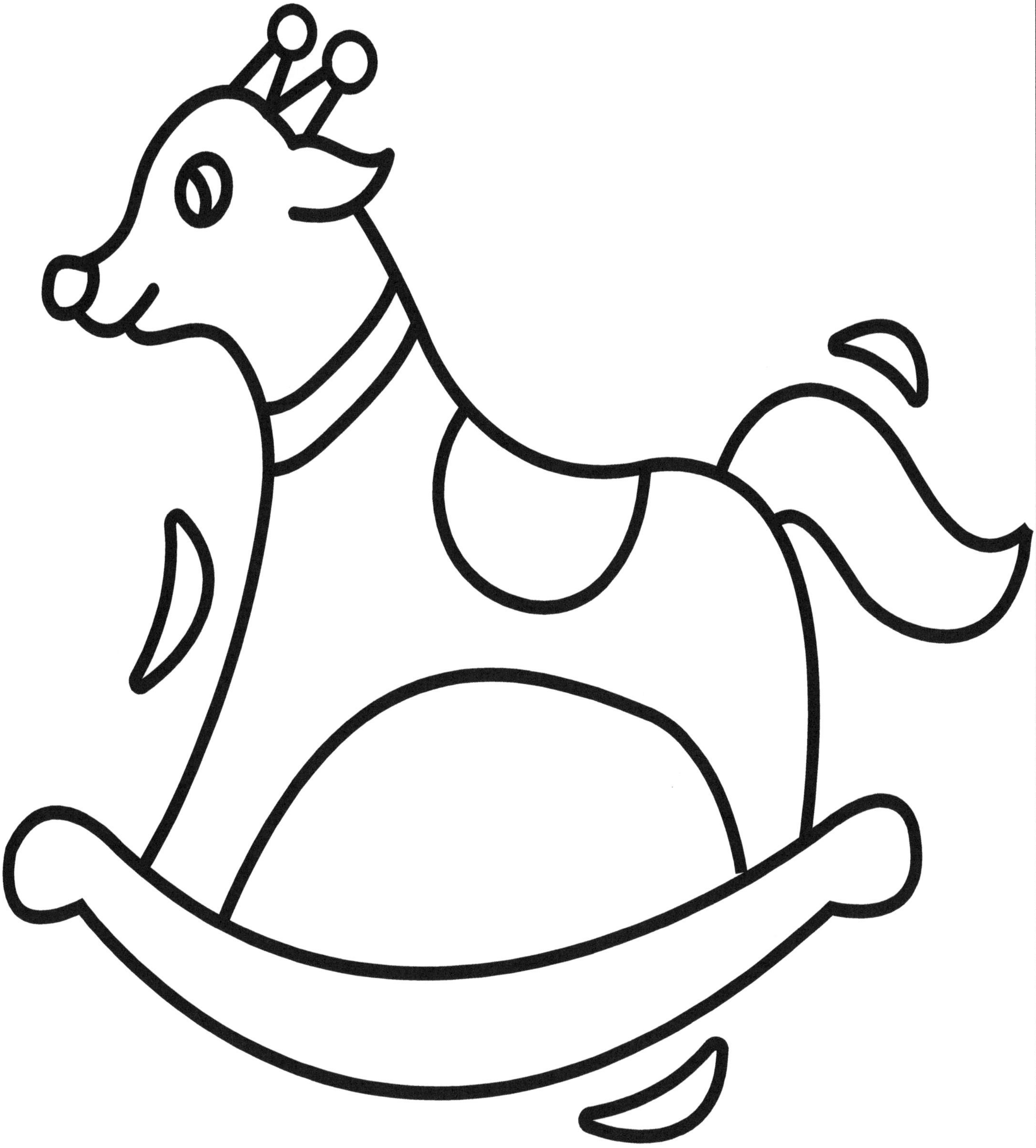

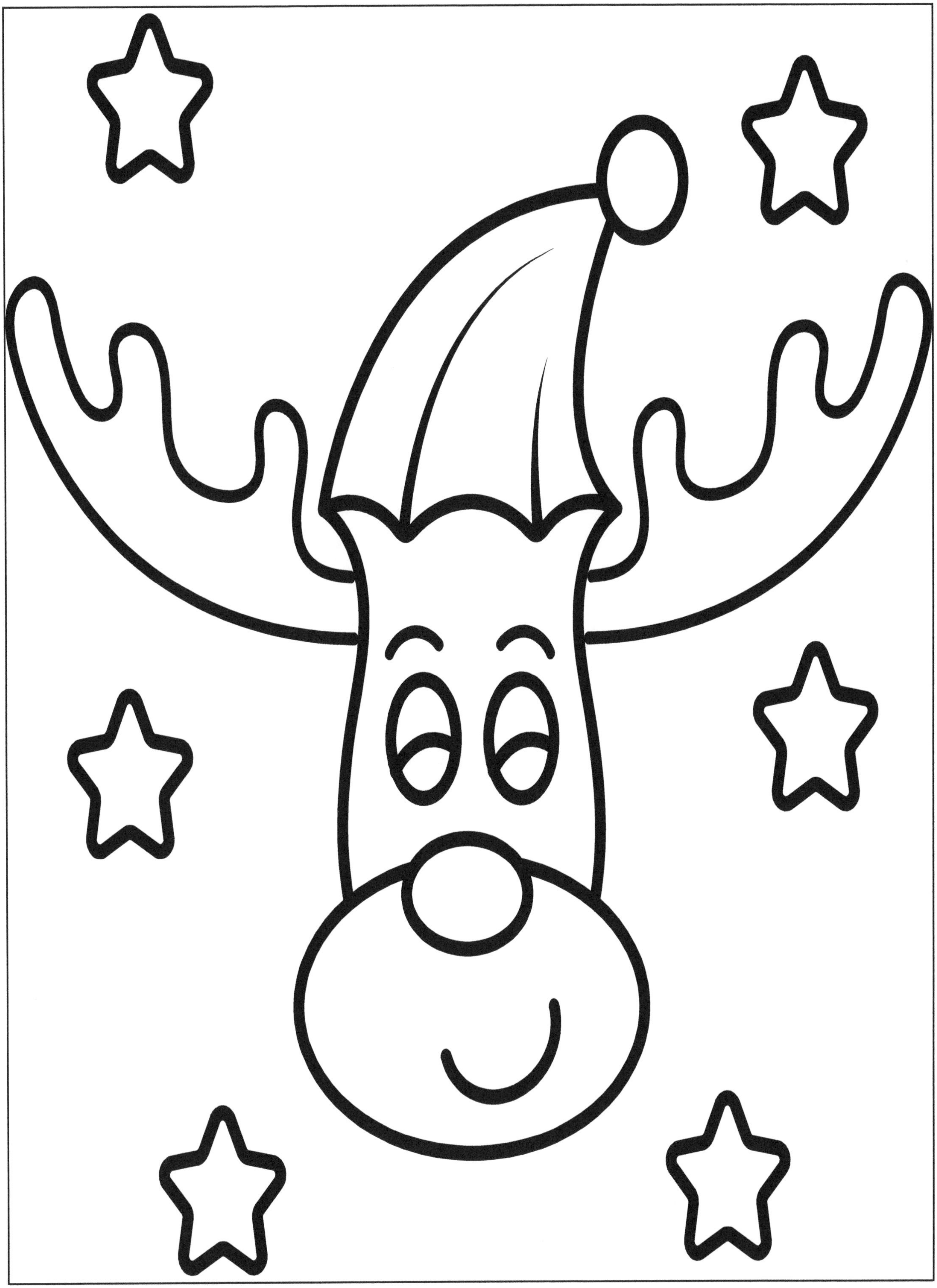

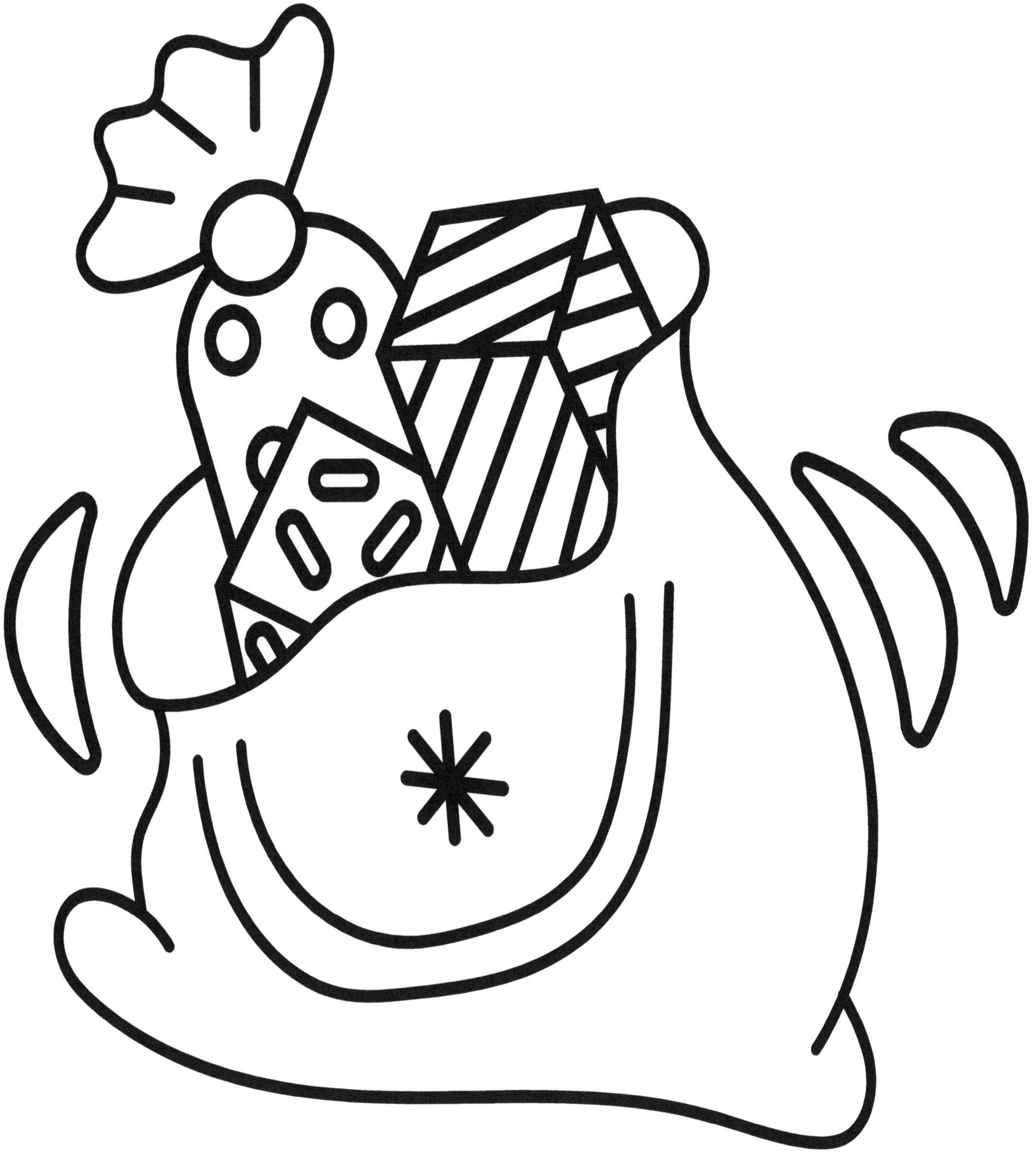

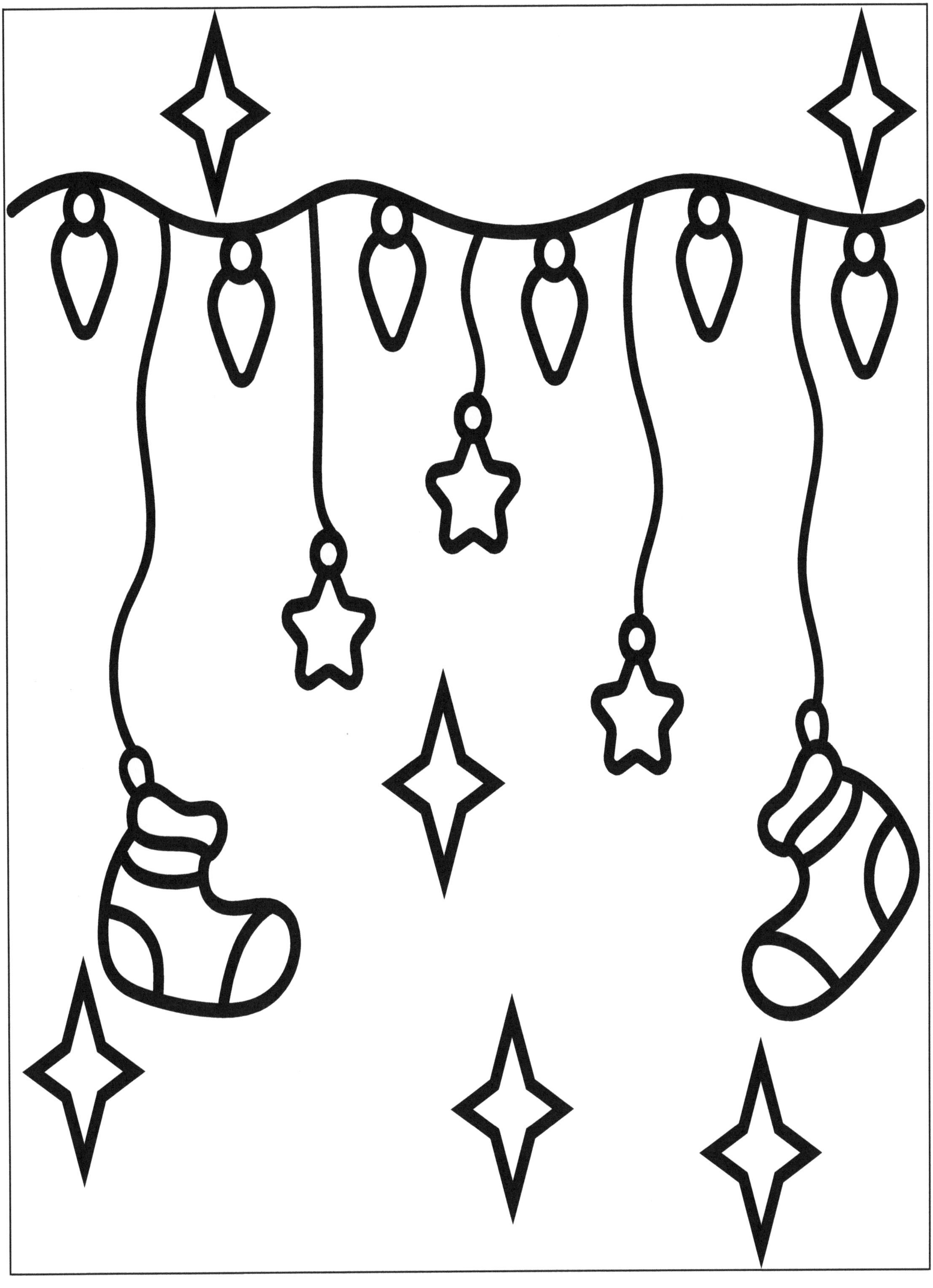

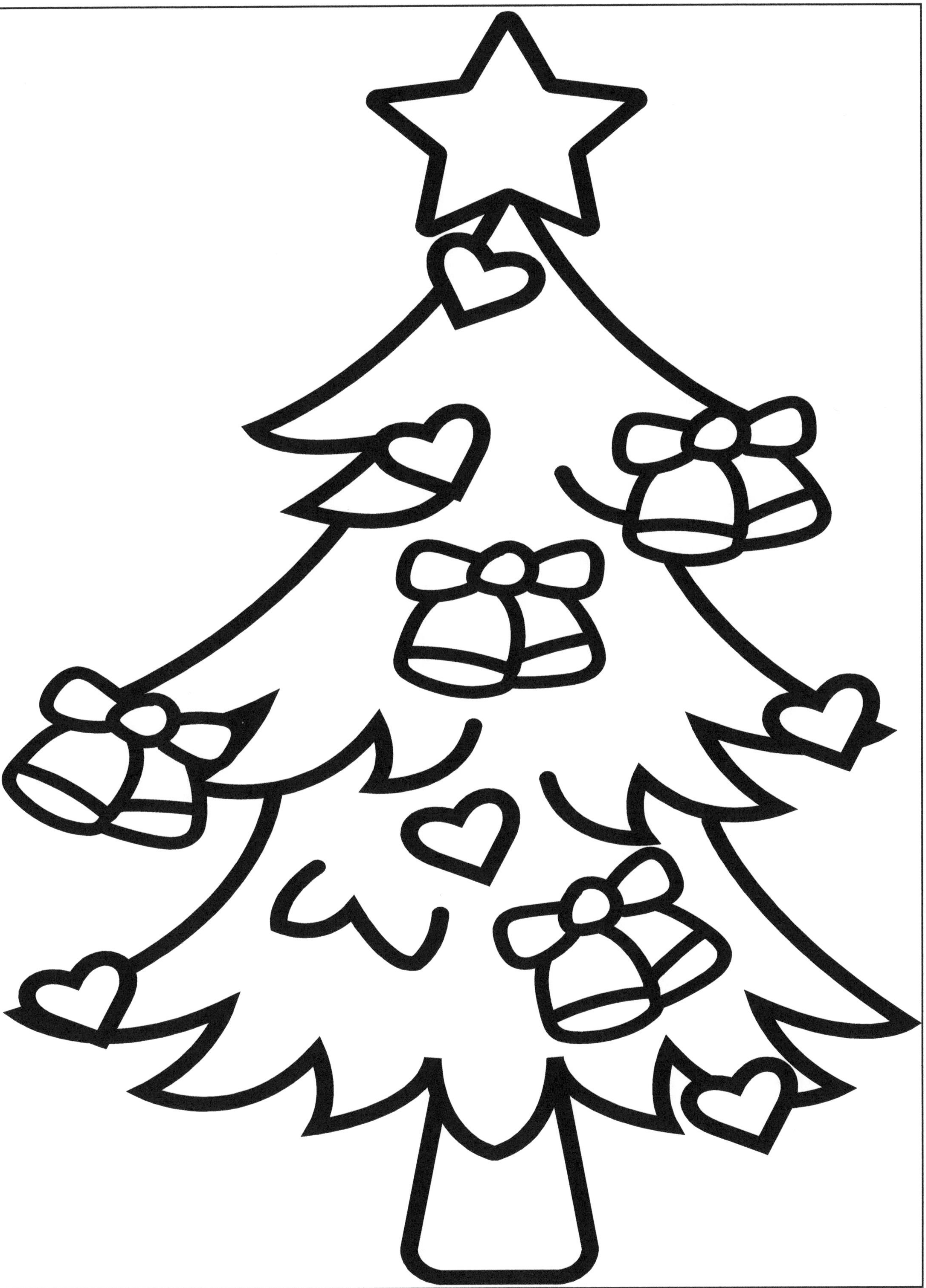

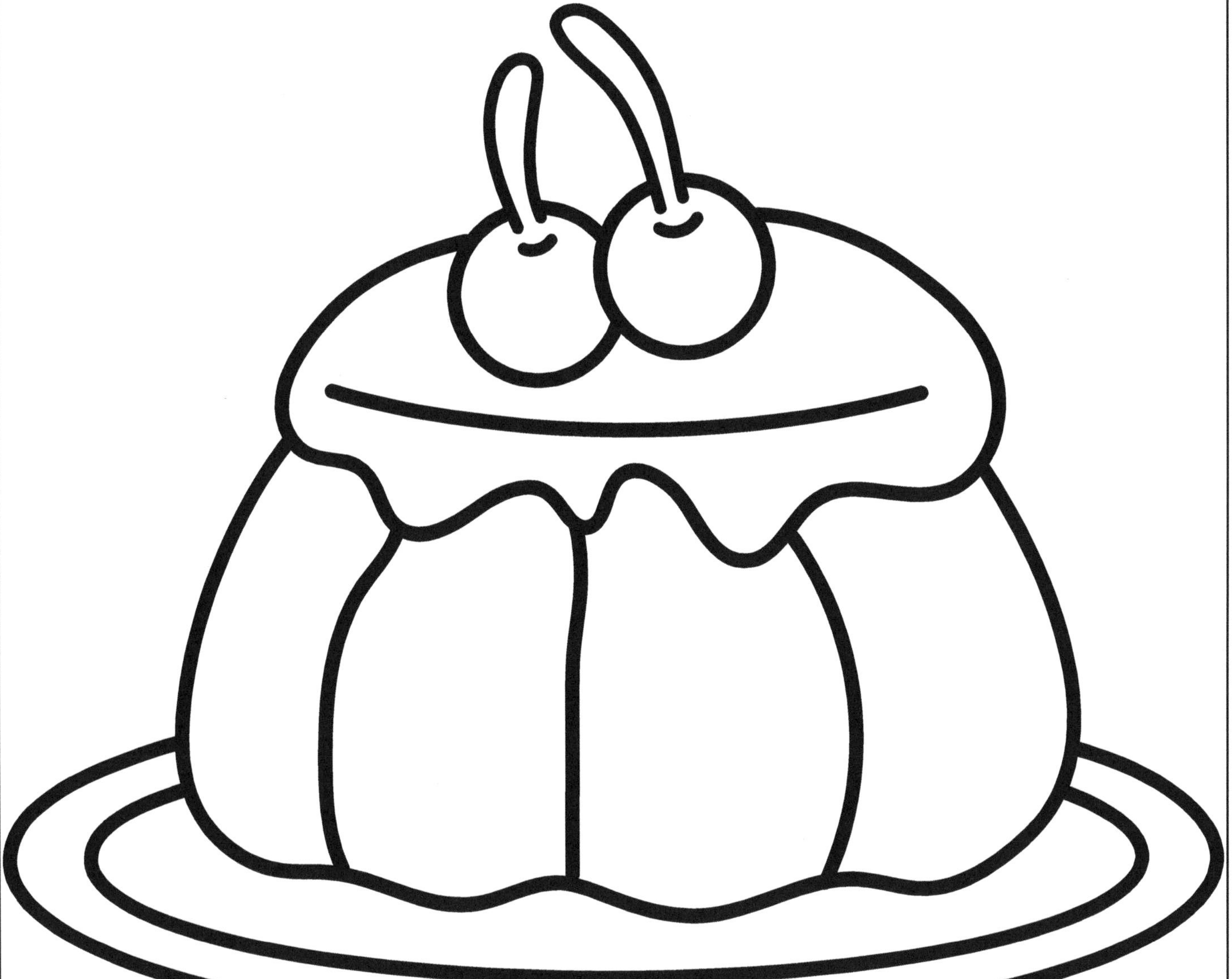

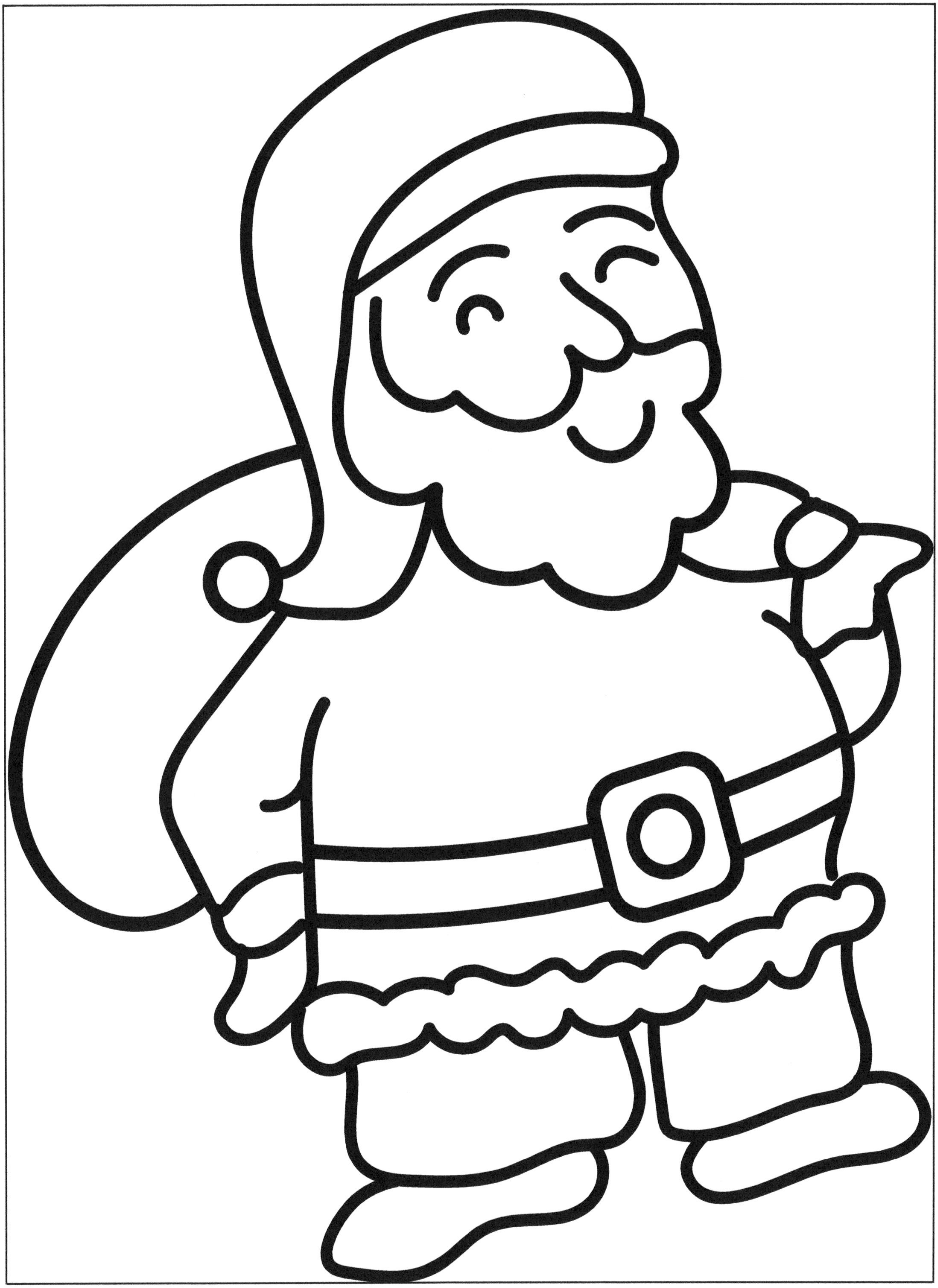

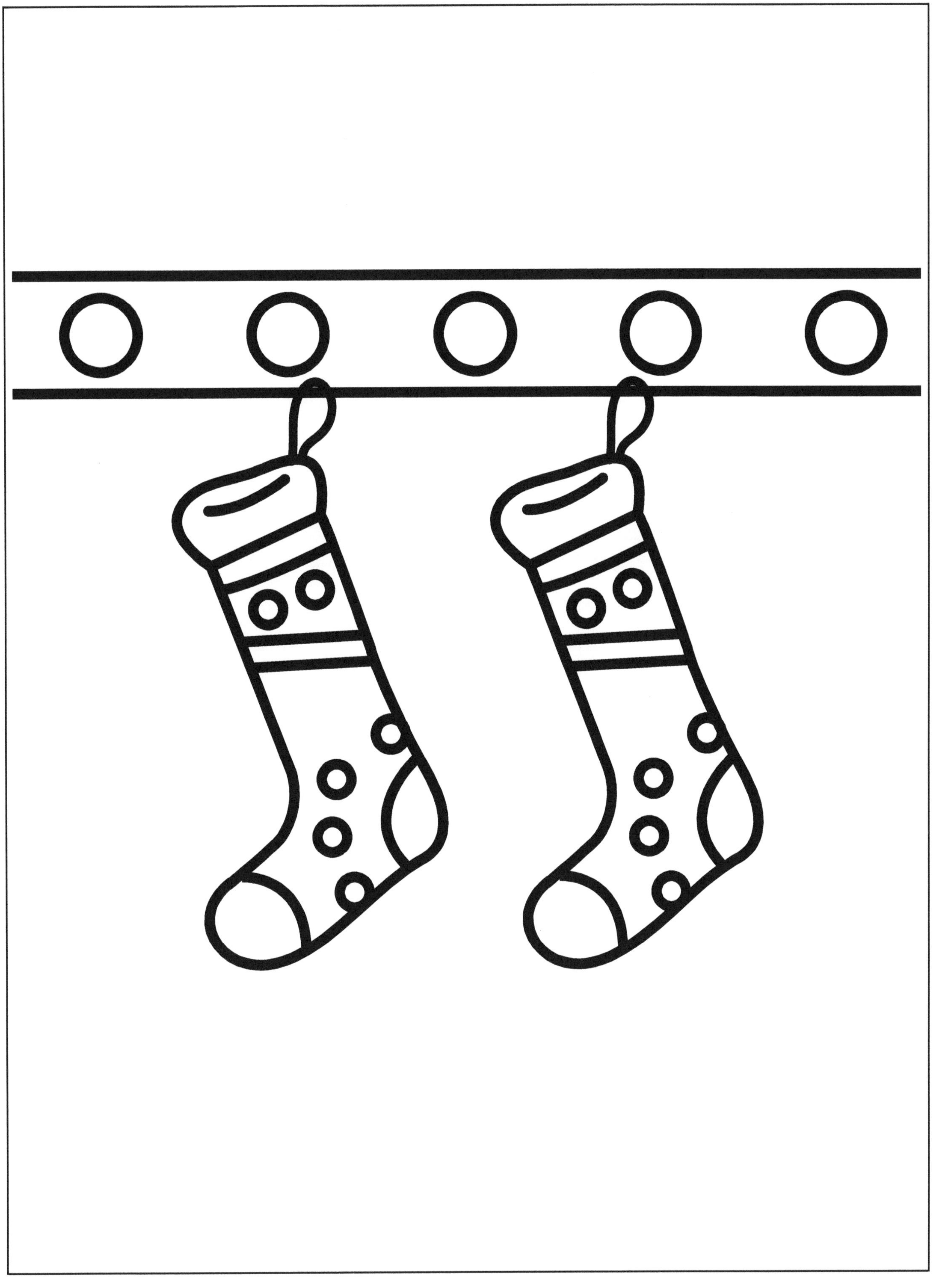

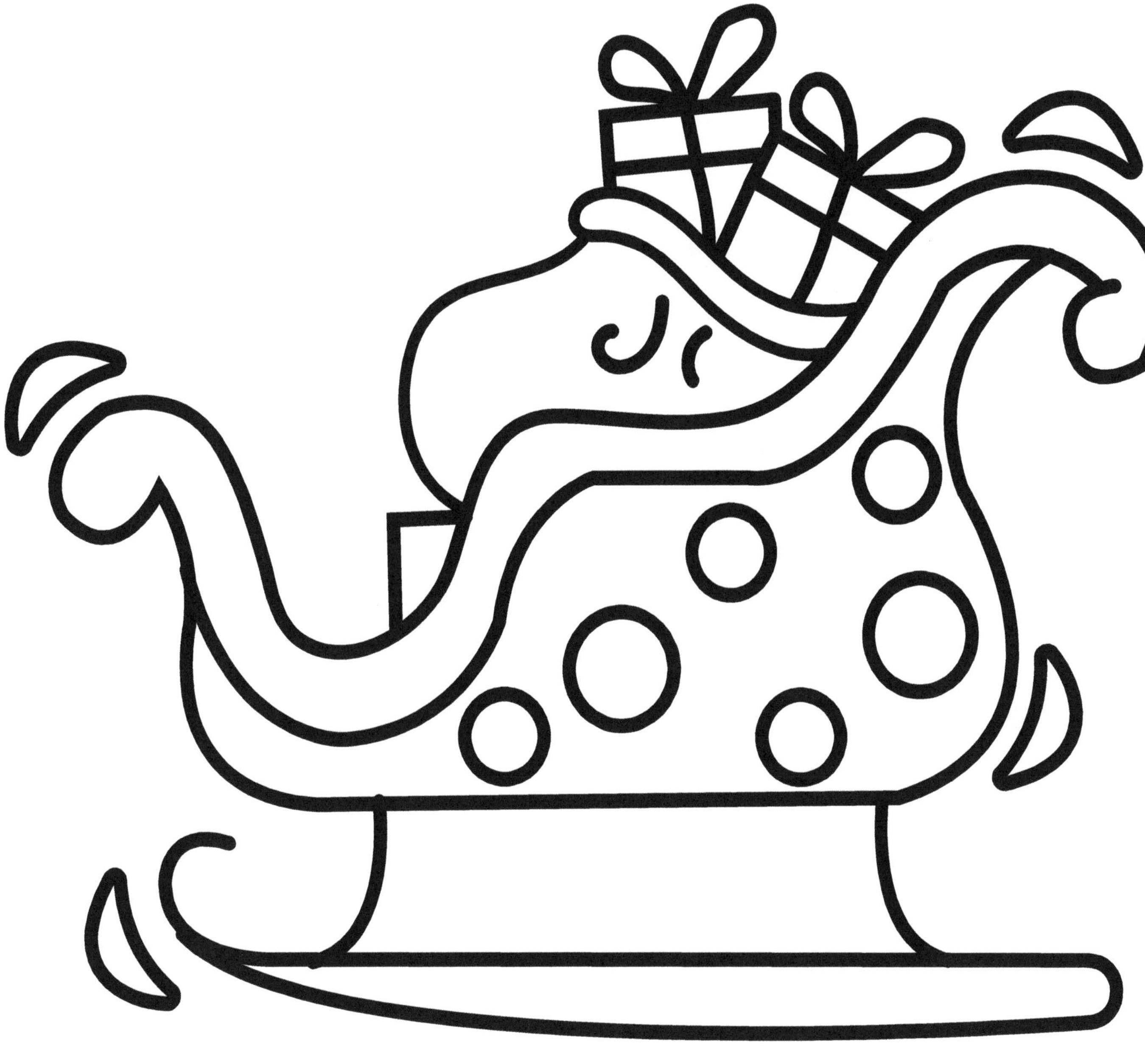

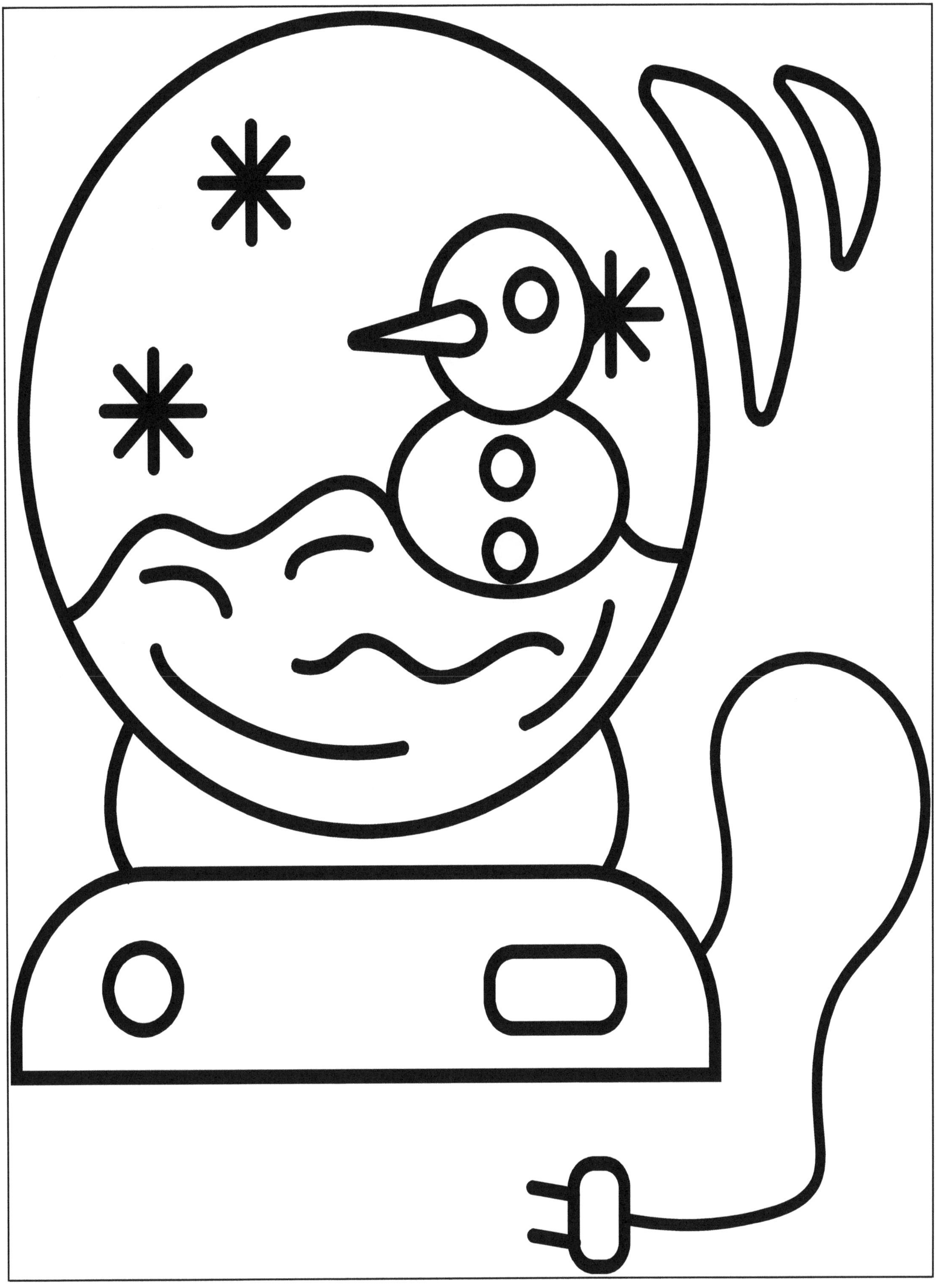

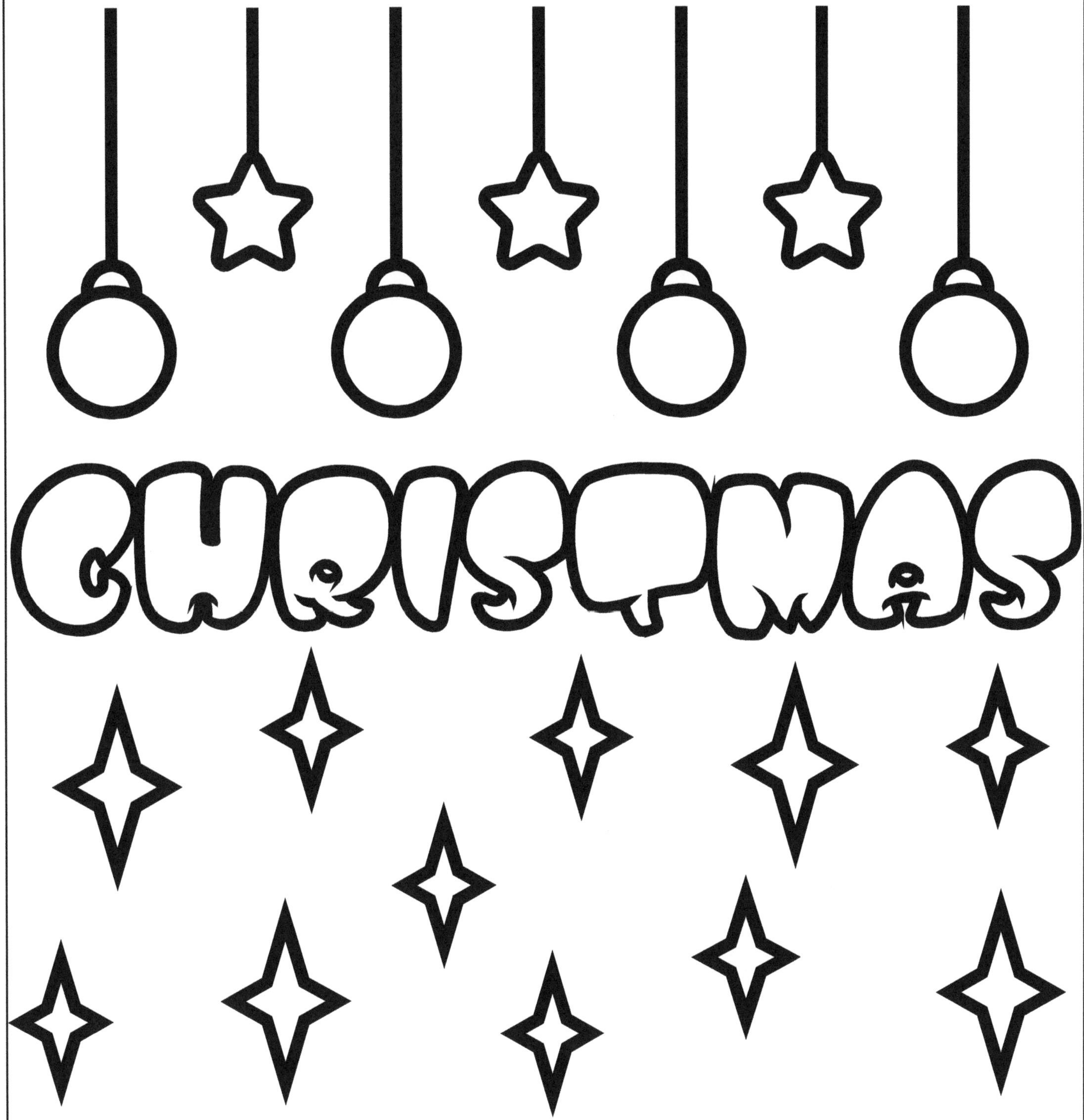
CHRISTMAS

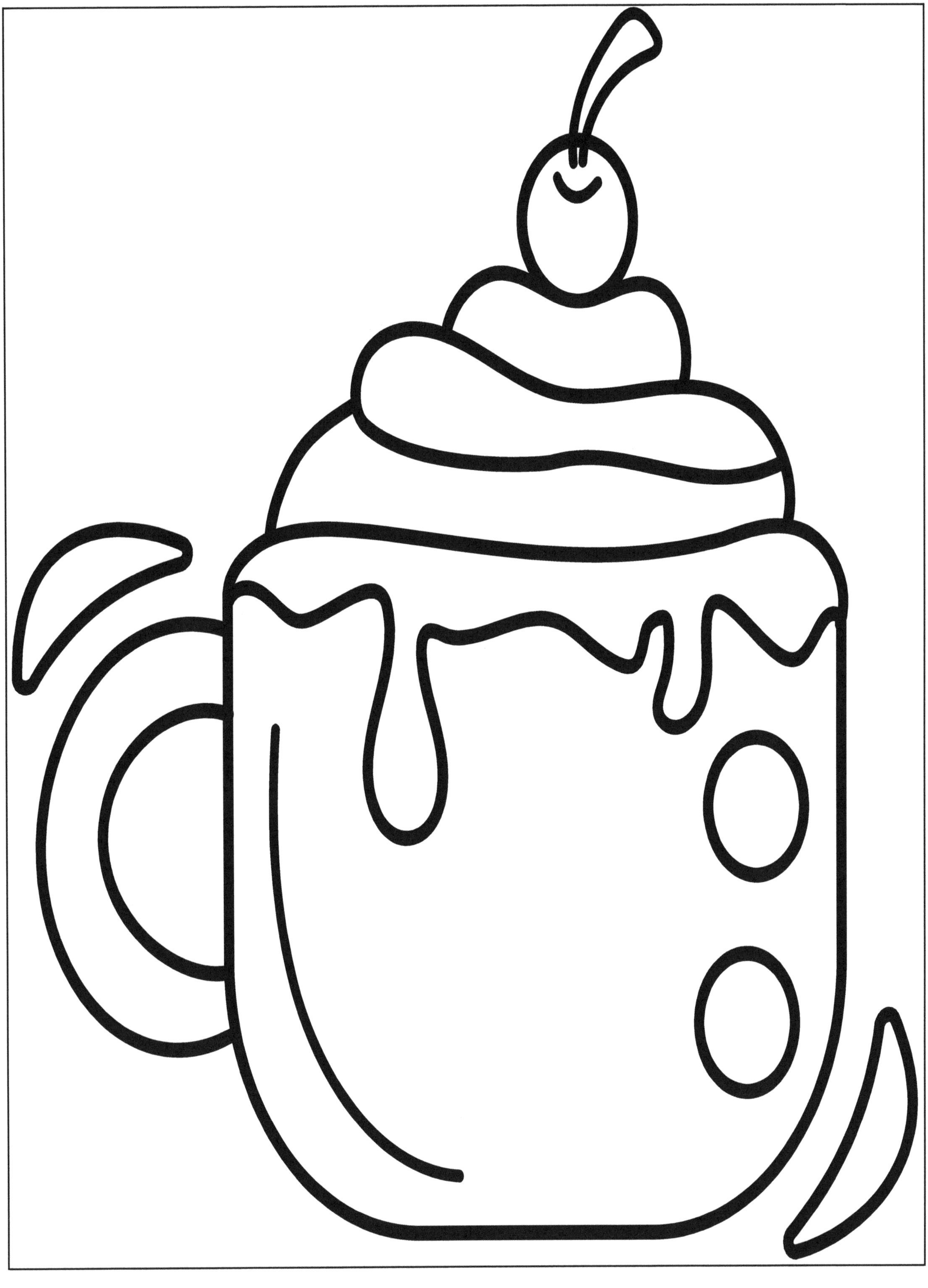

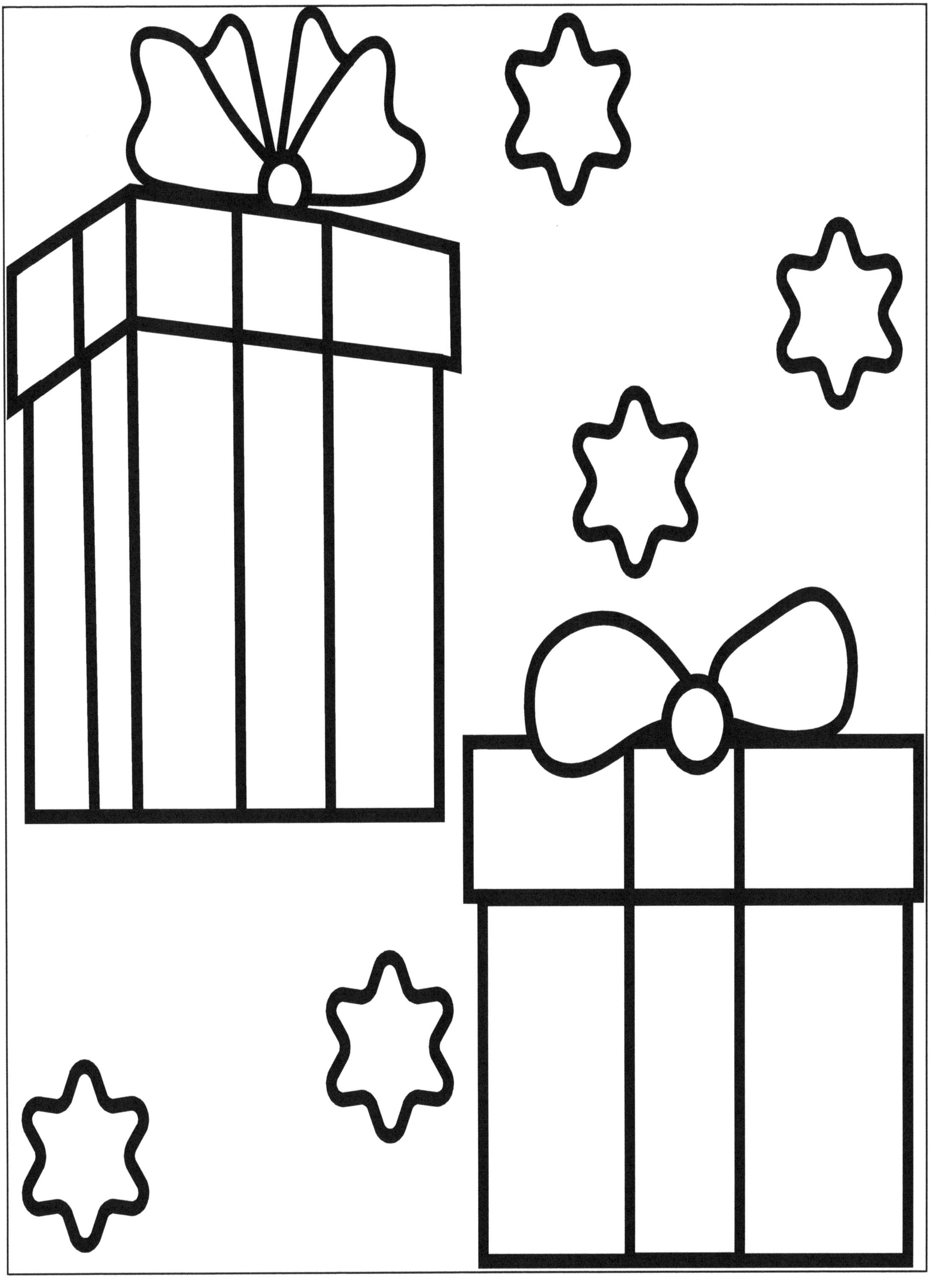

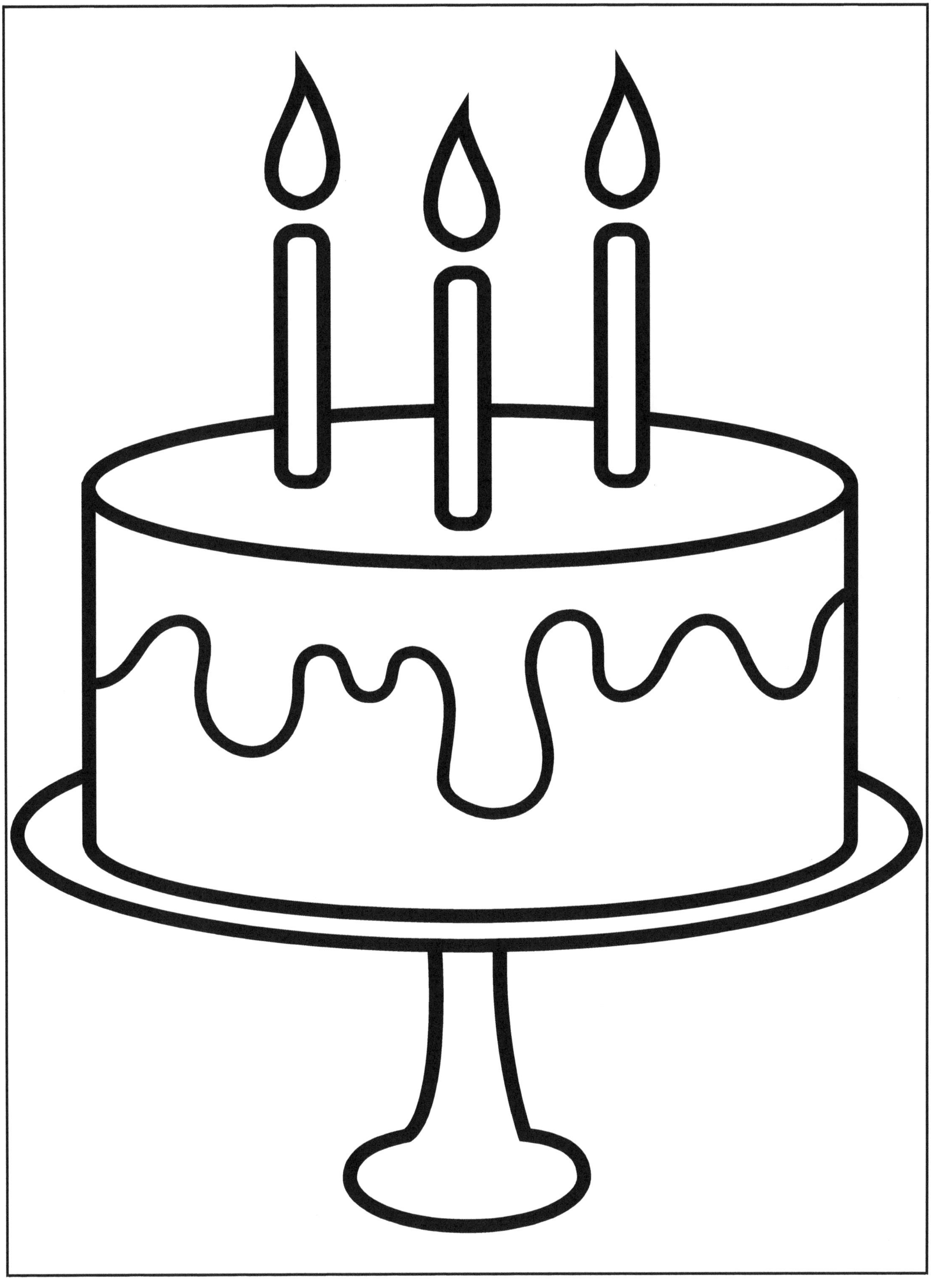

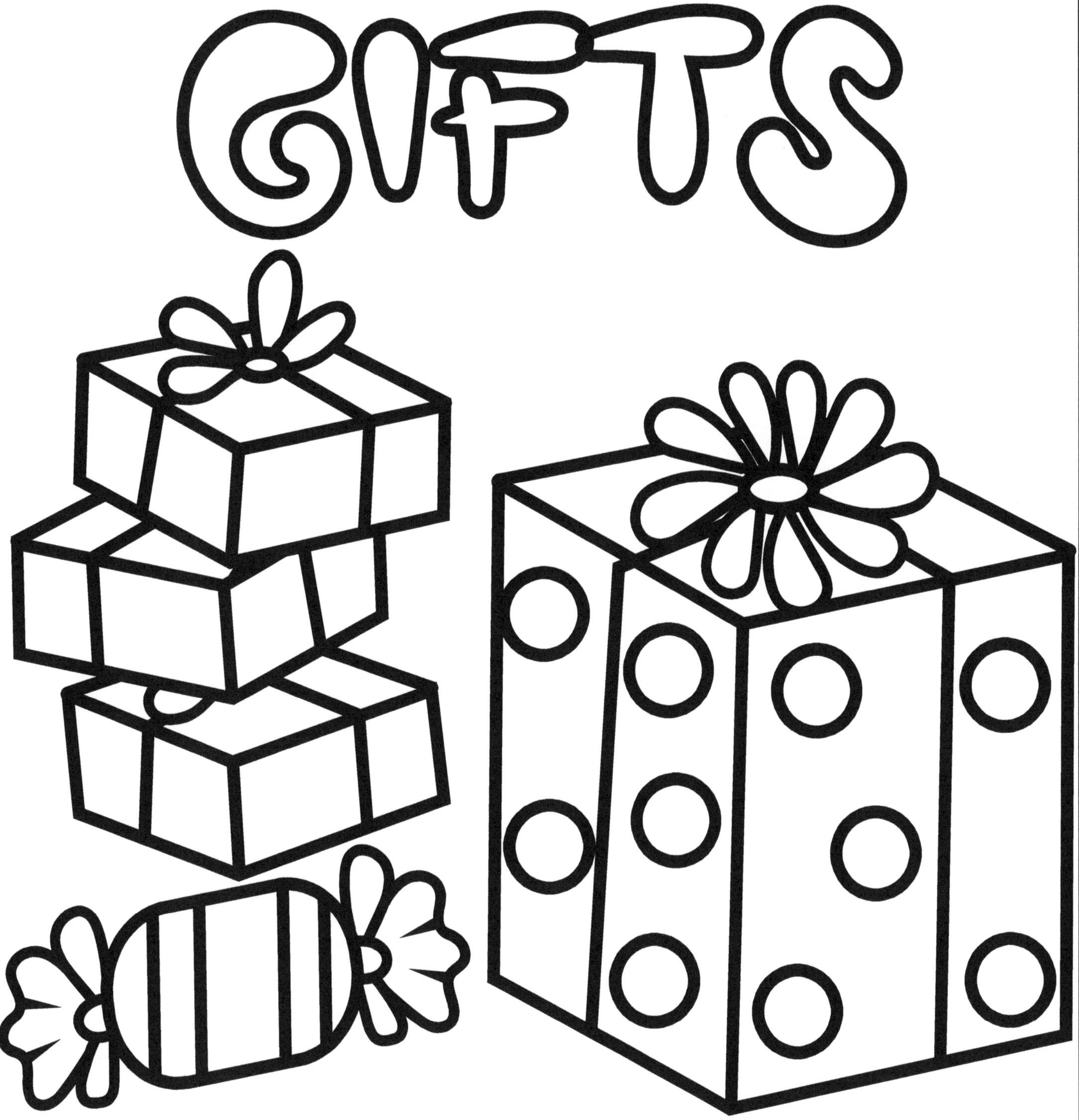
GIFTS

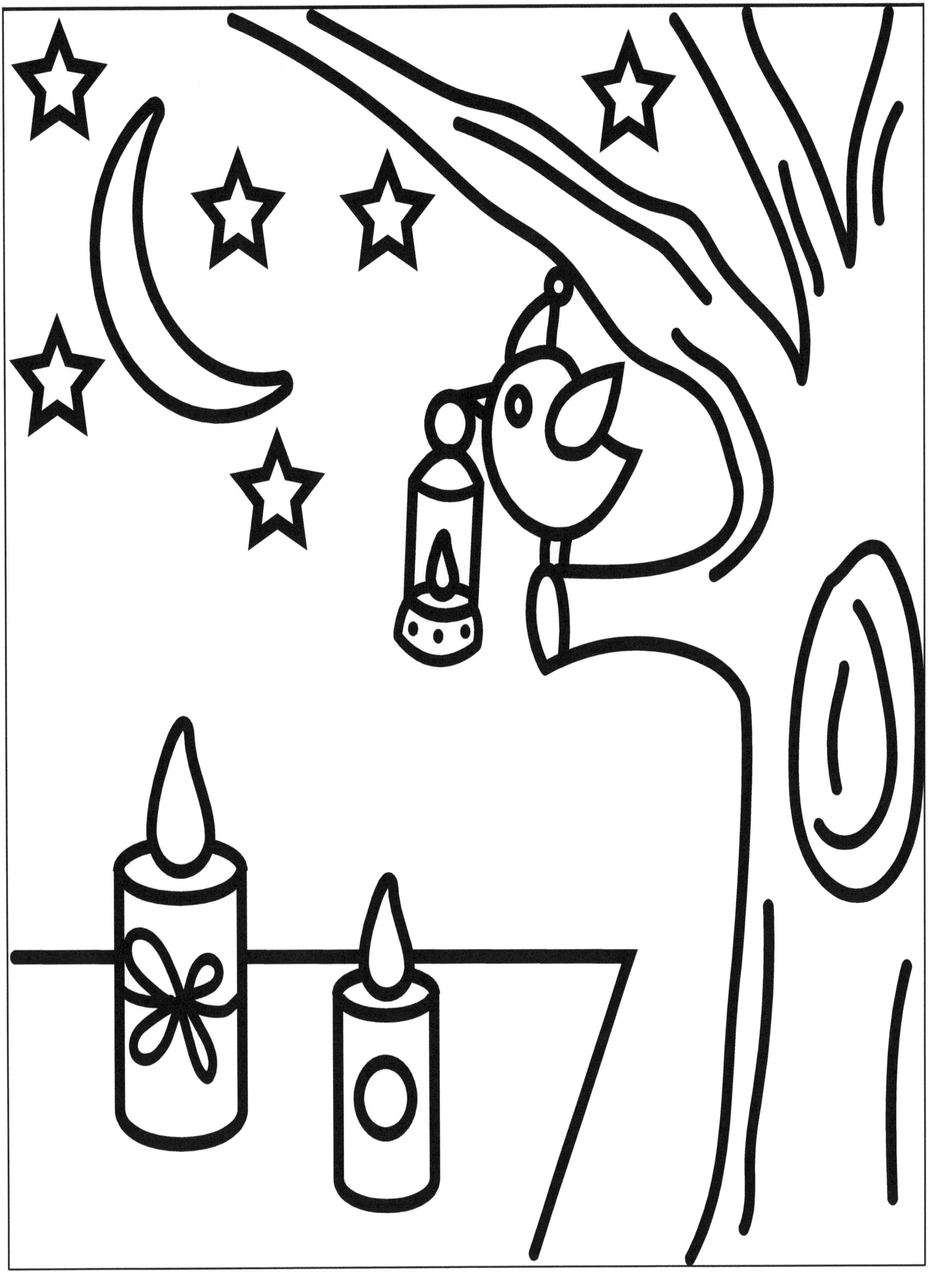

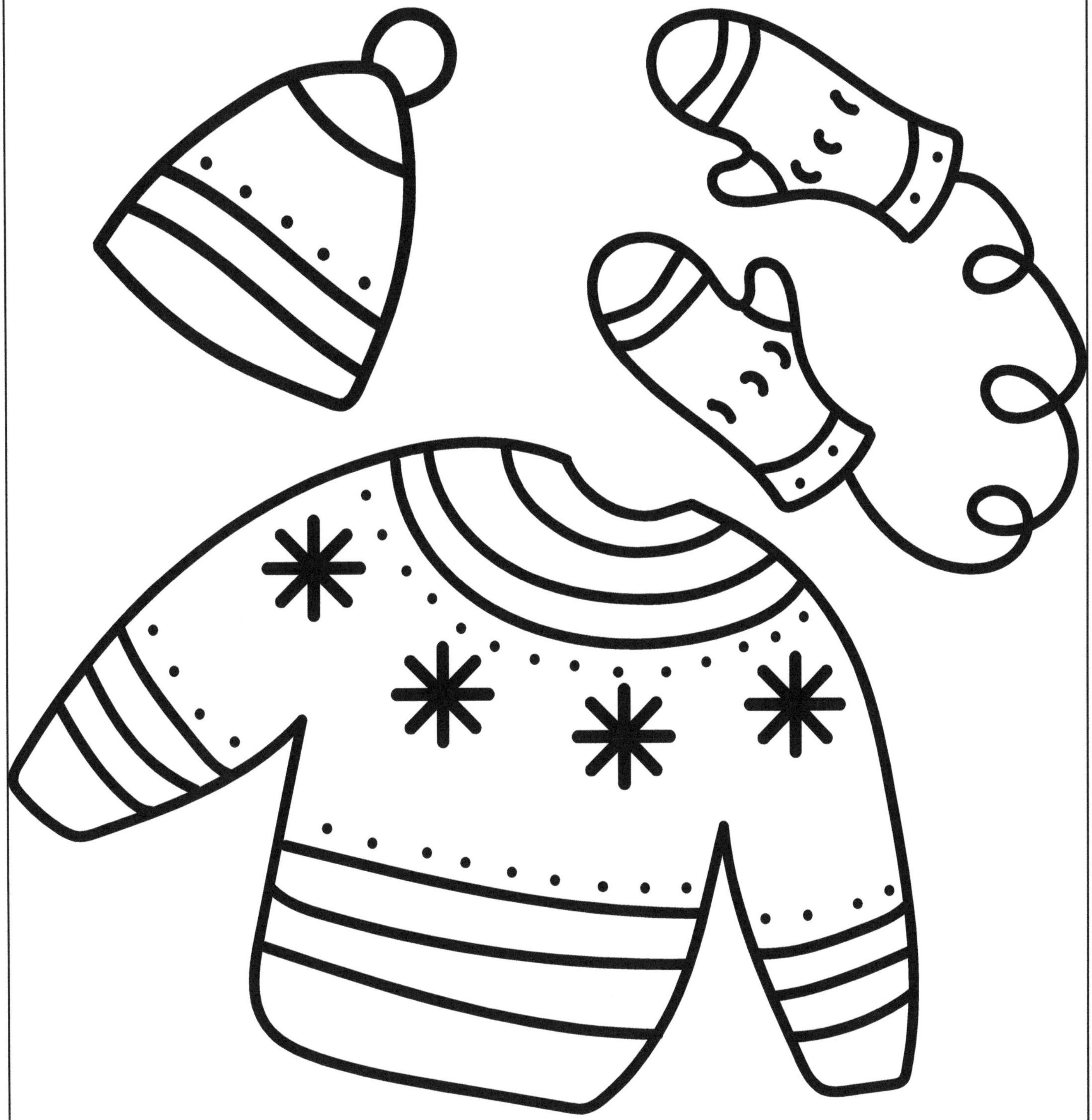

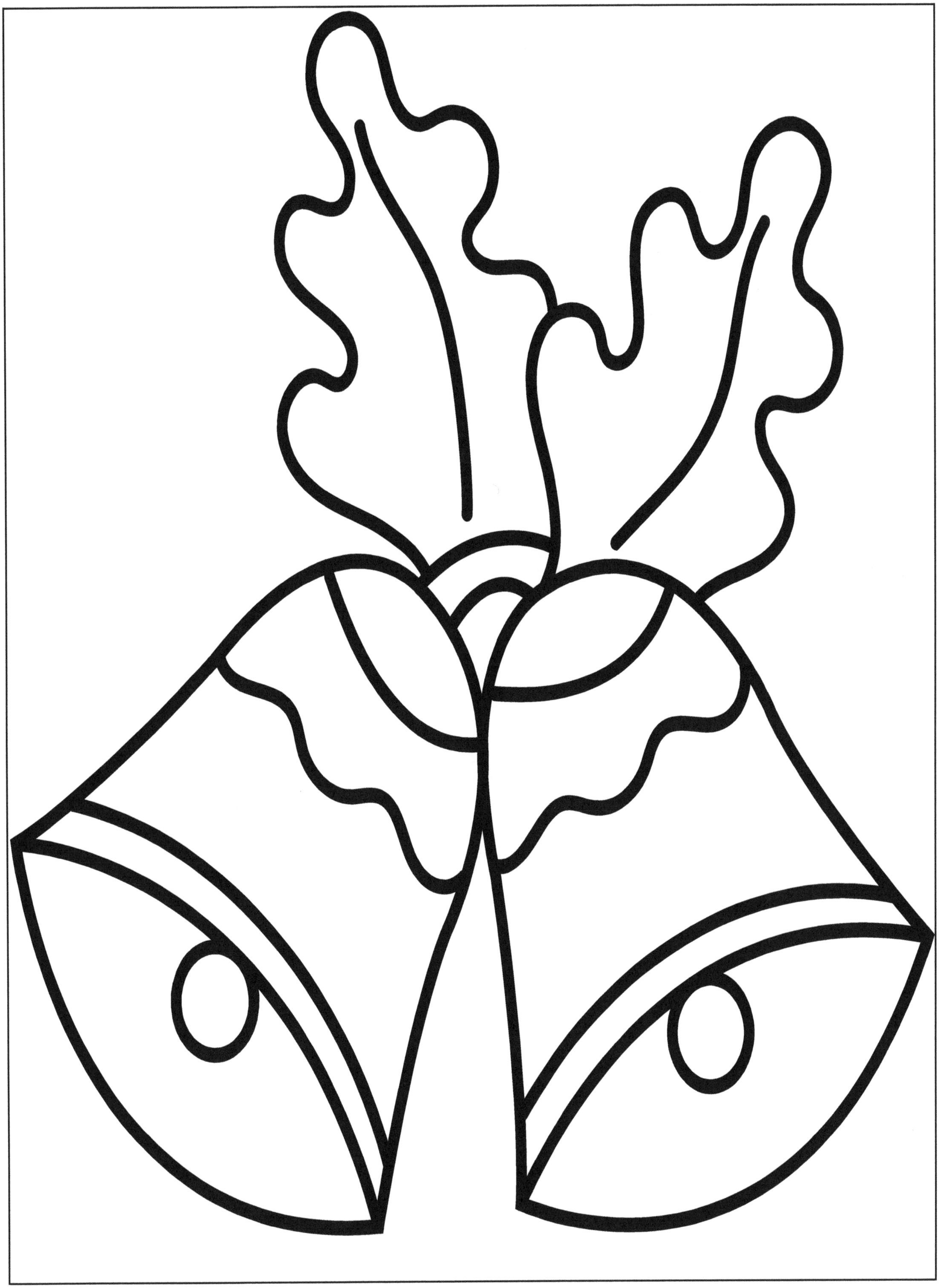

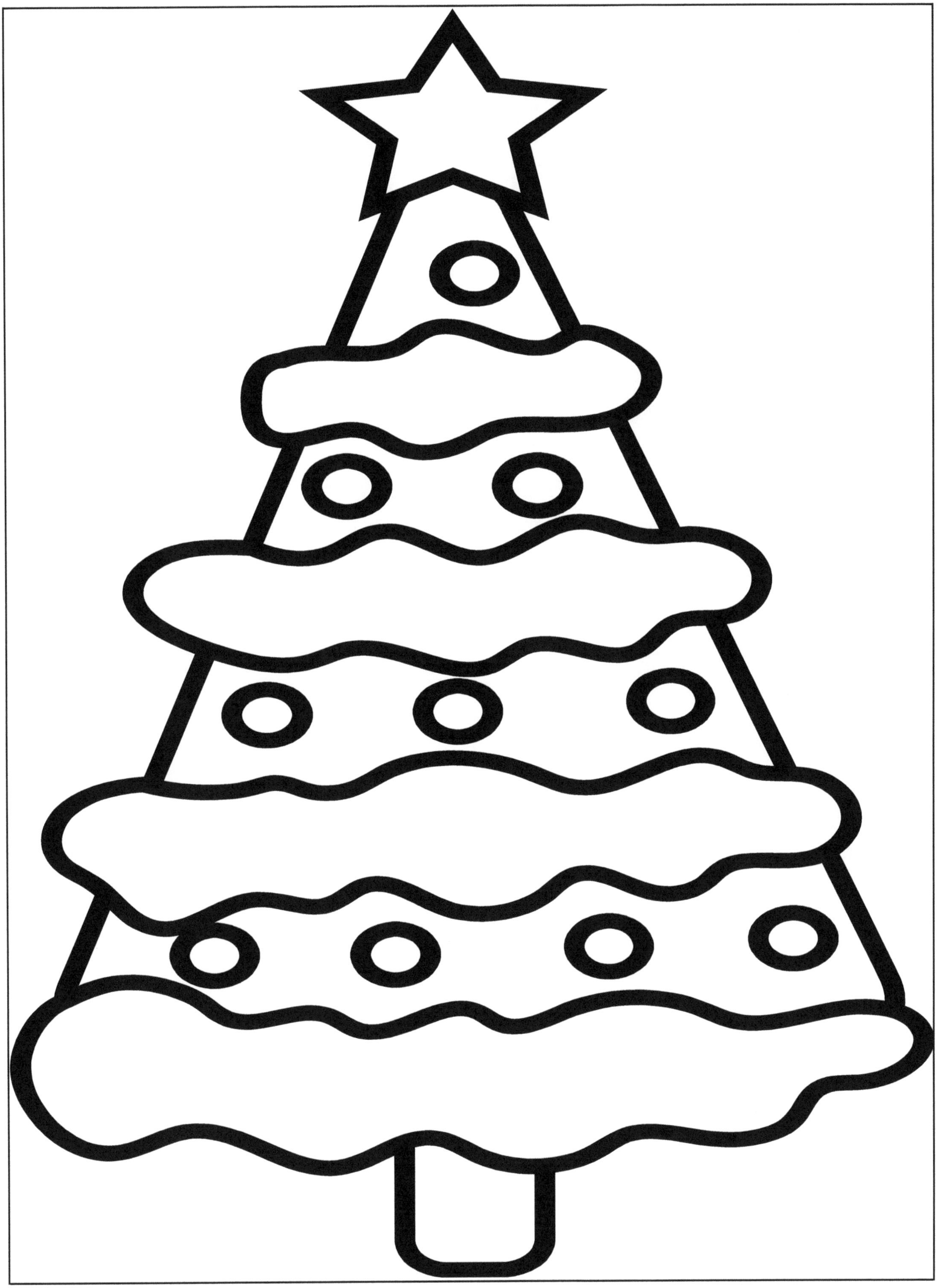

Merry
Christmas

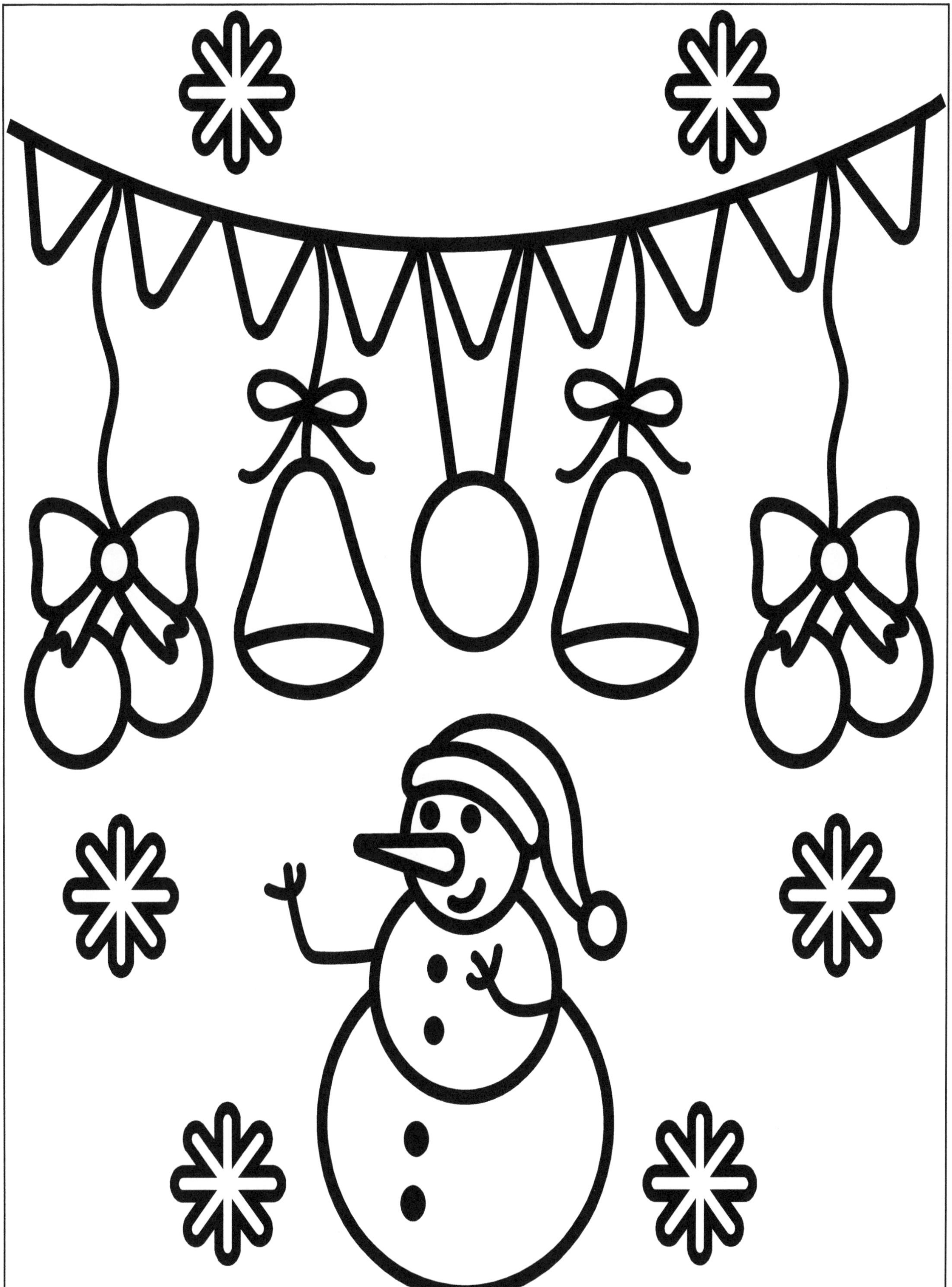

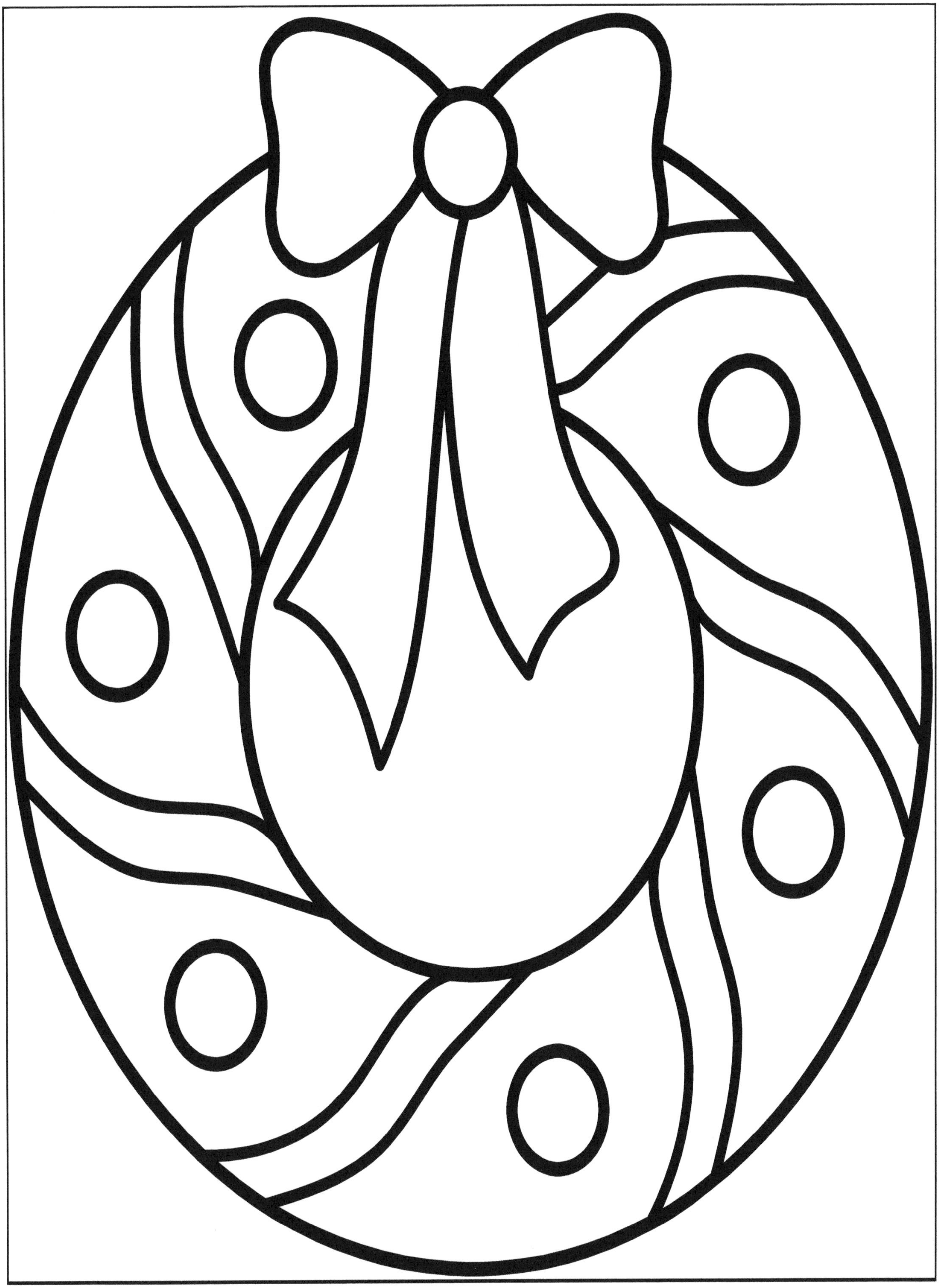

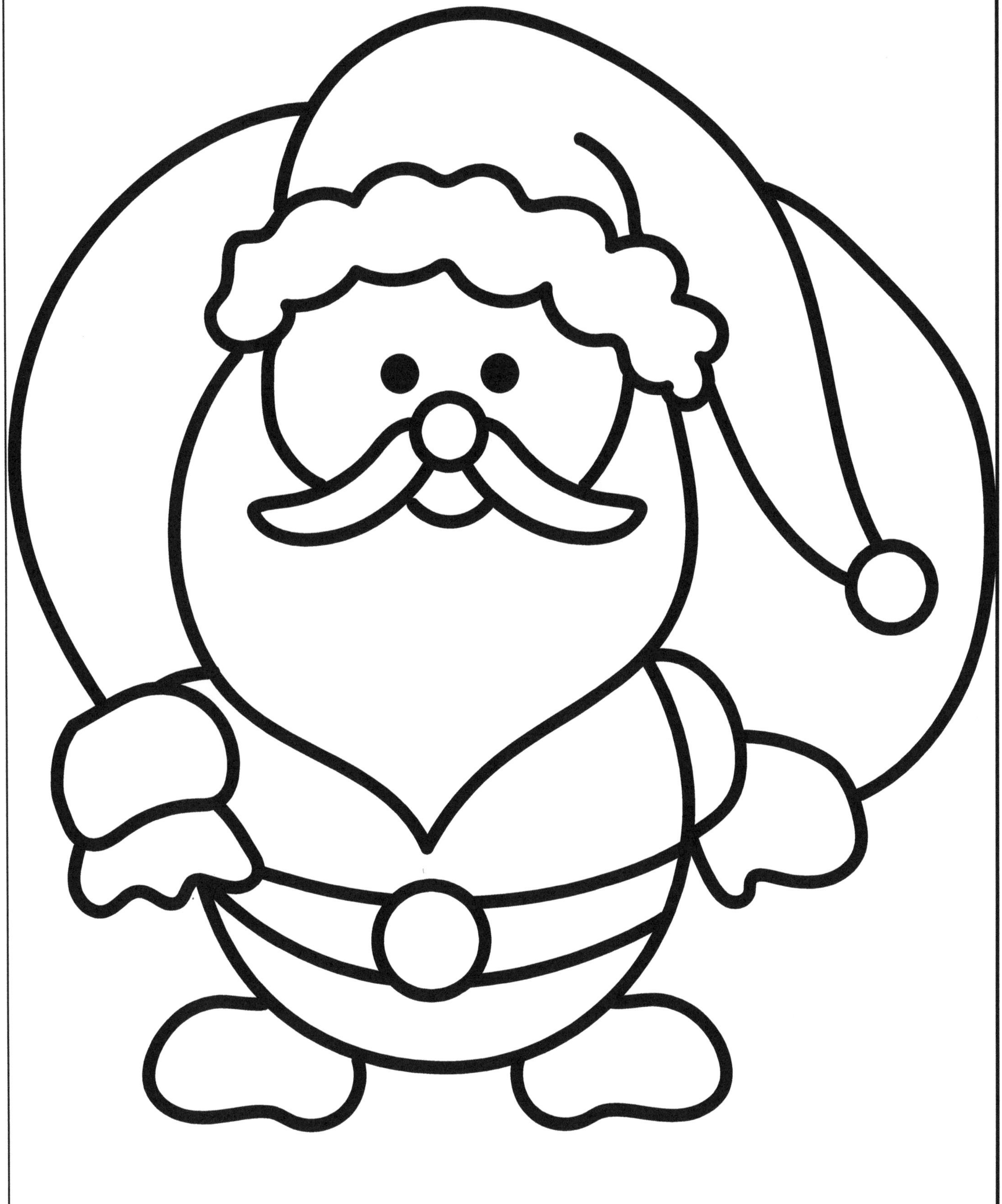

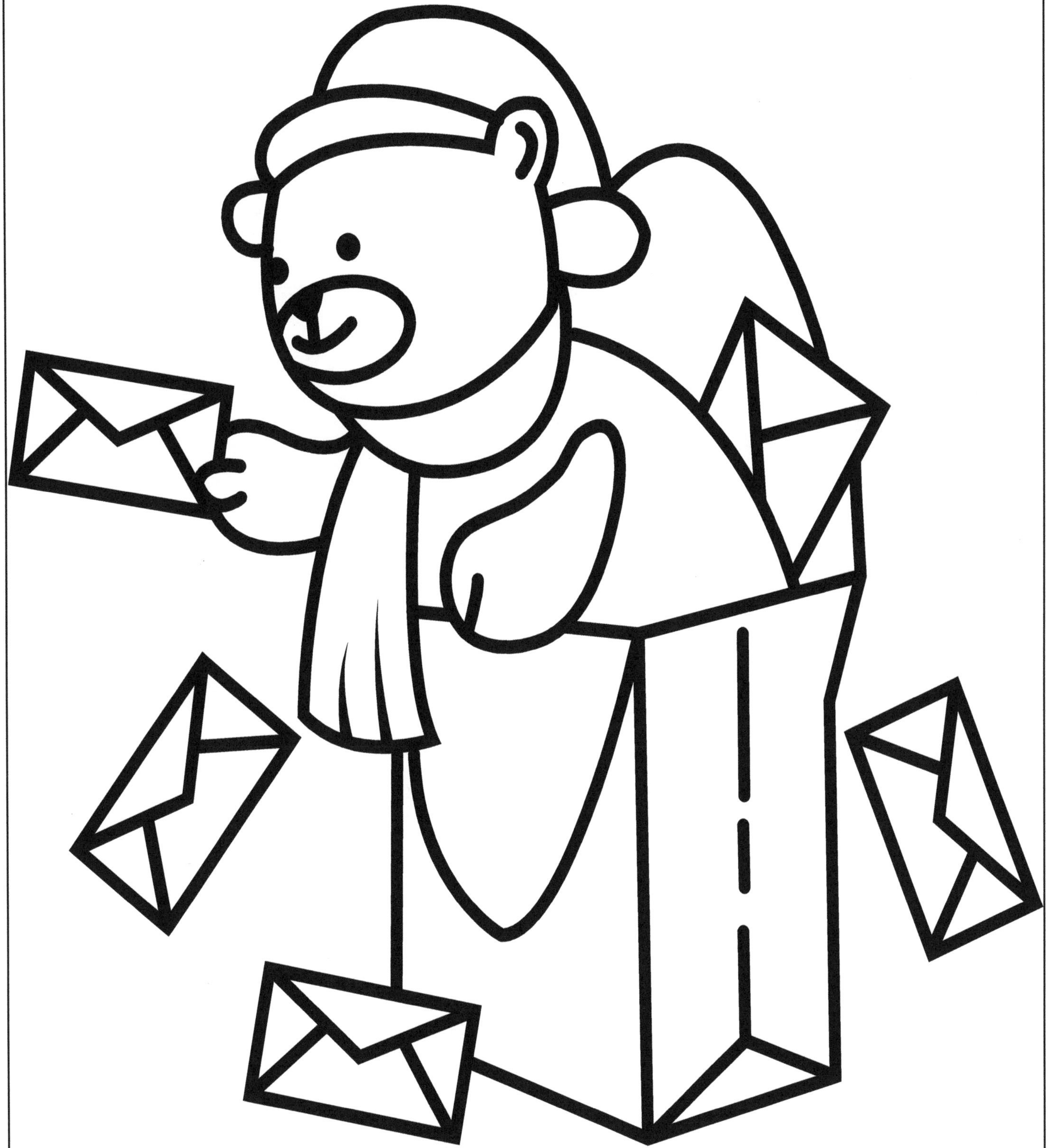

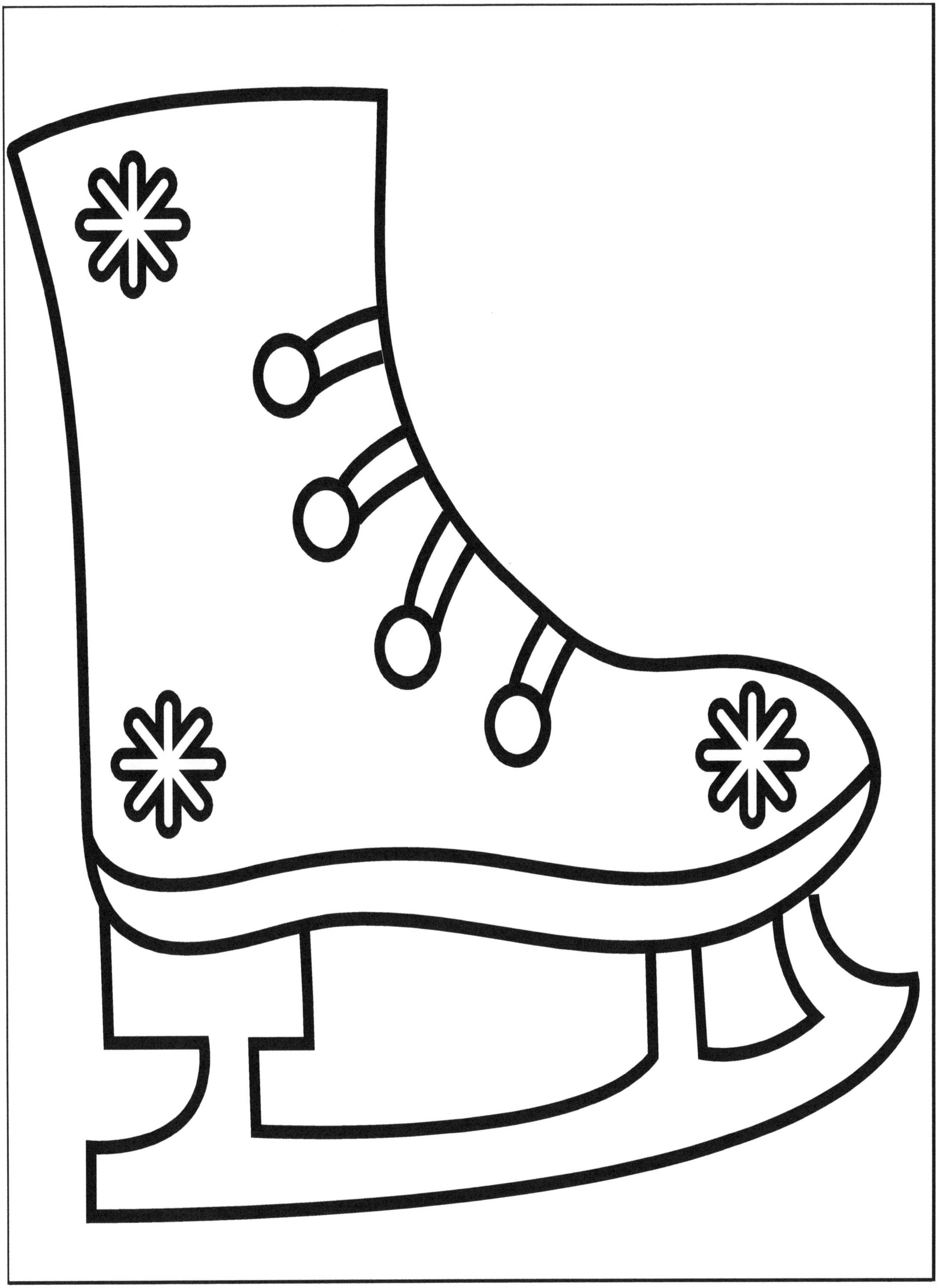

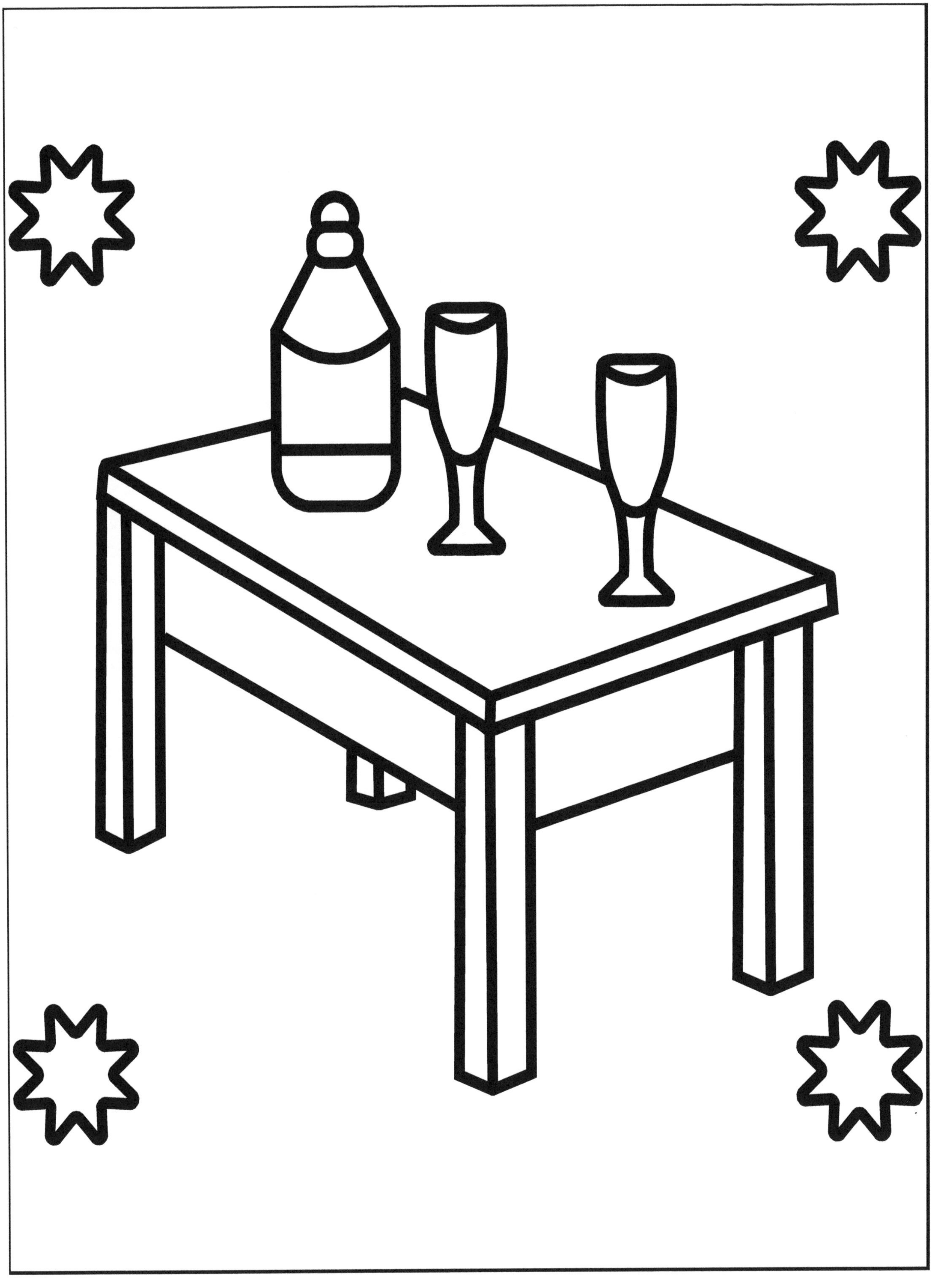

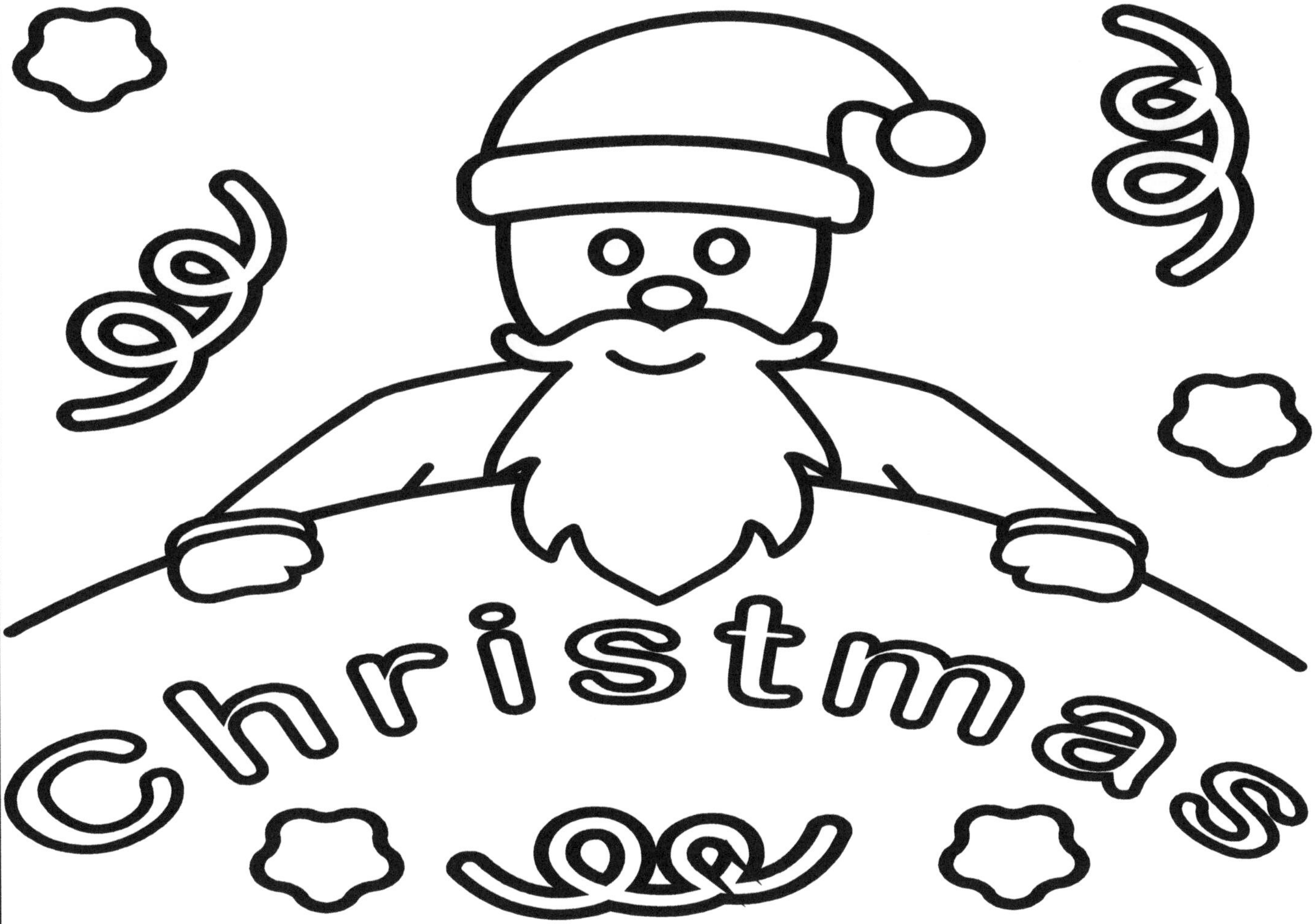
Christmas

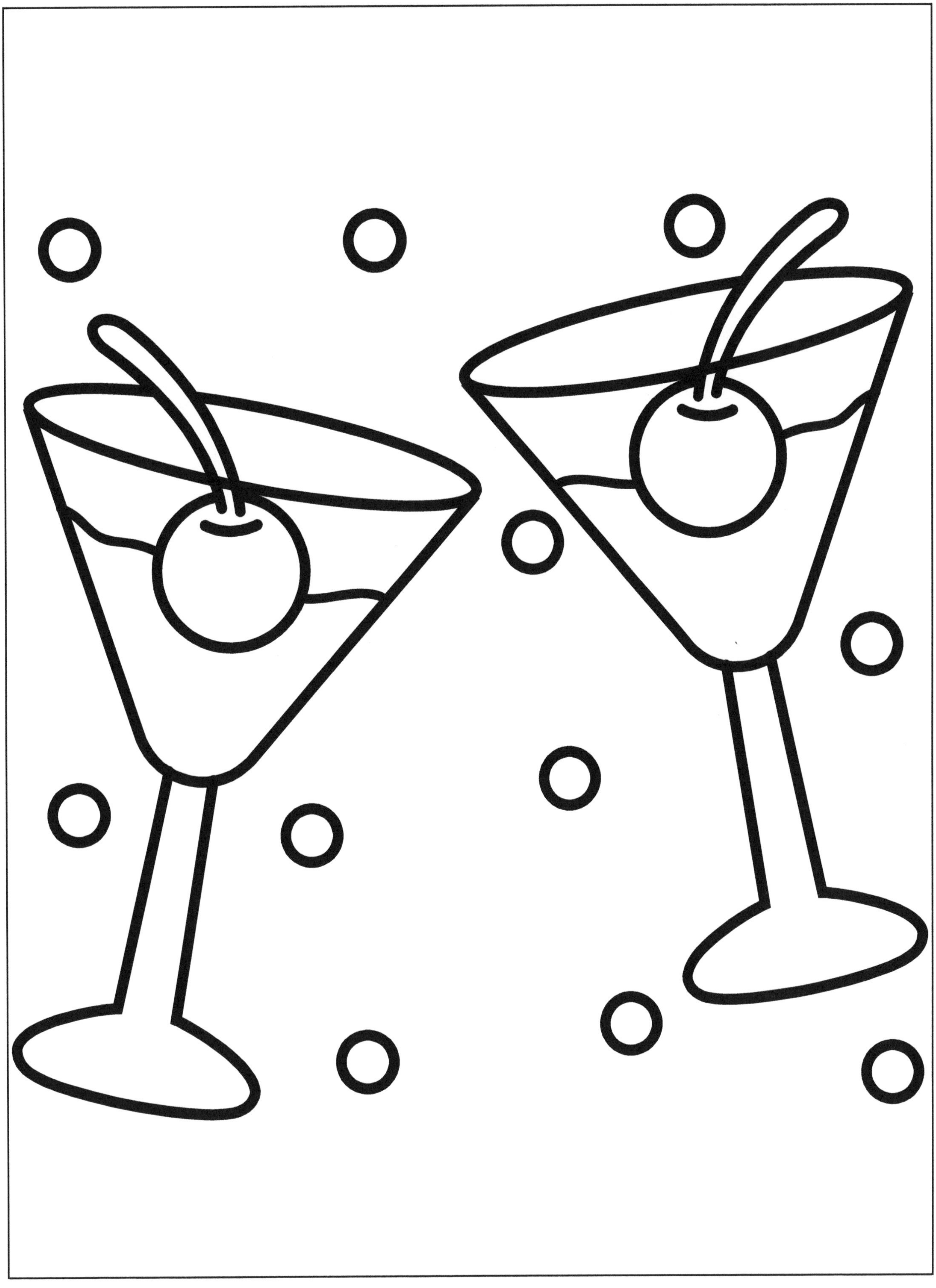

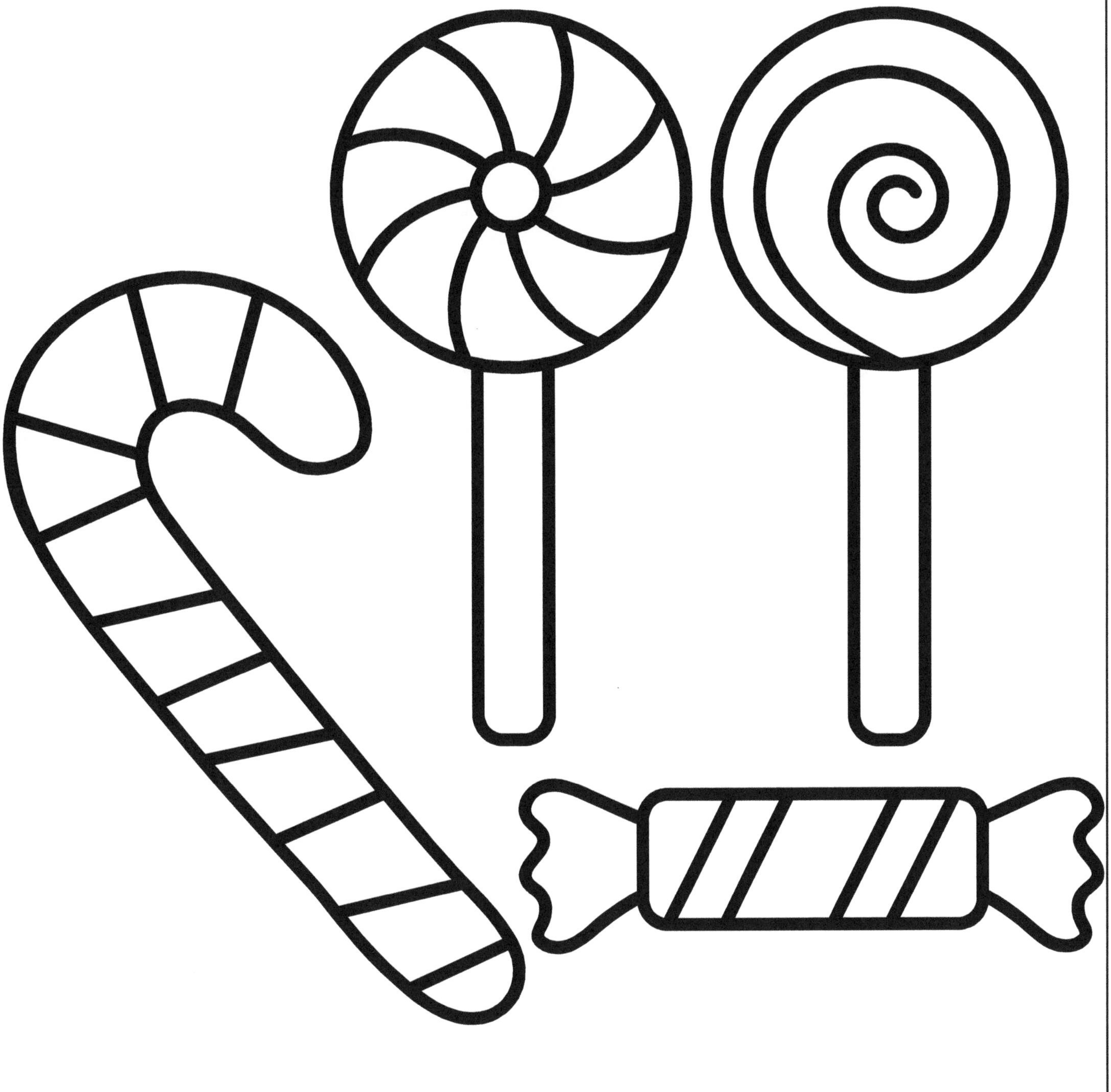

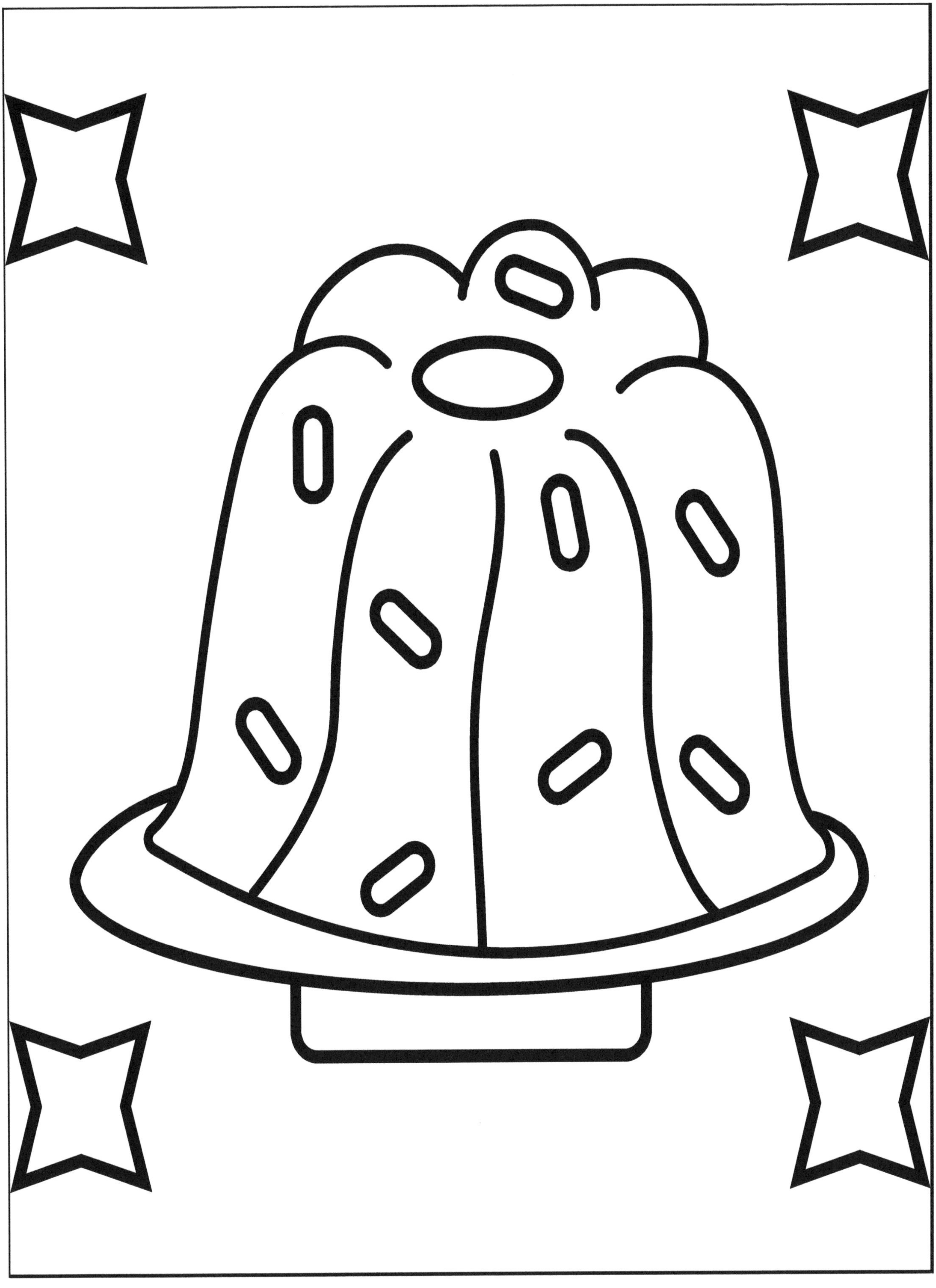

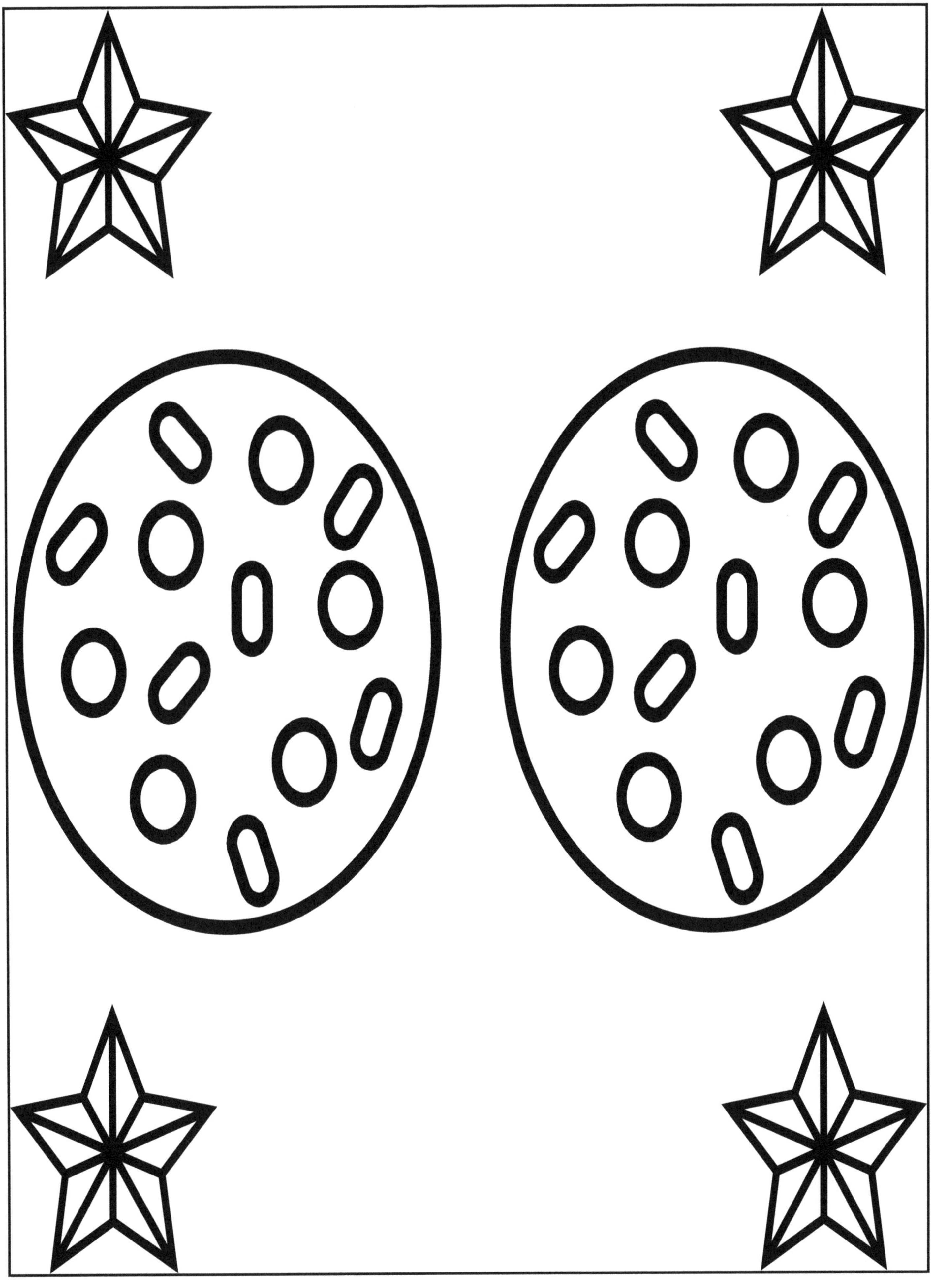

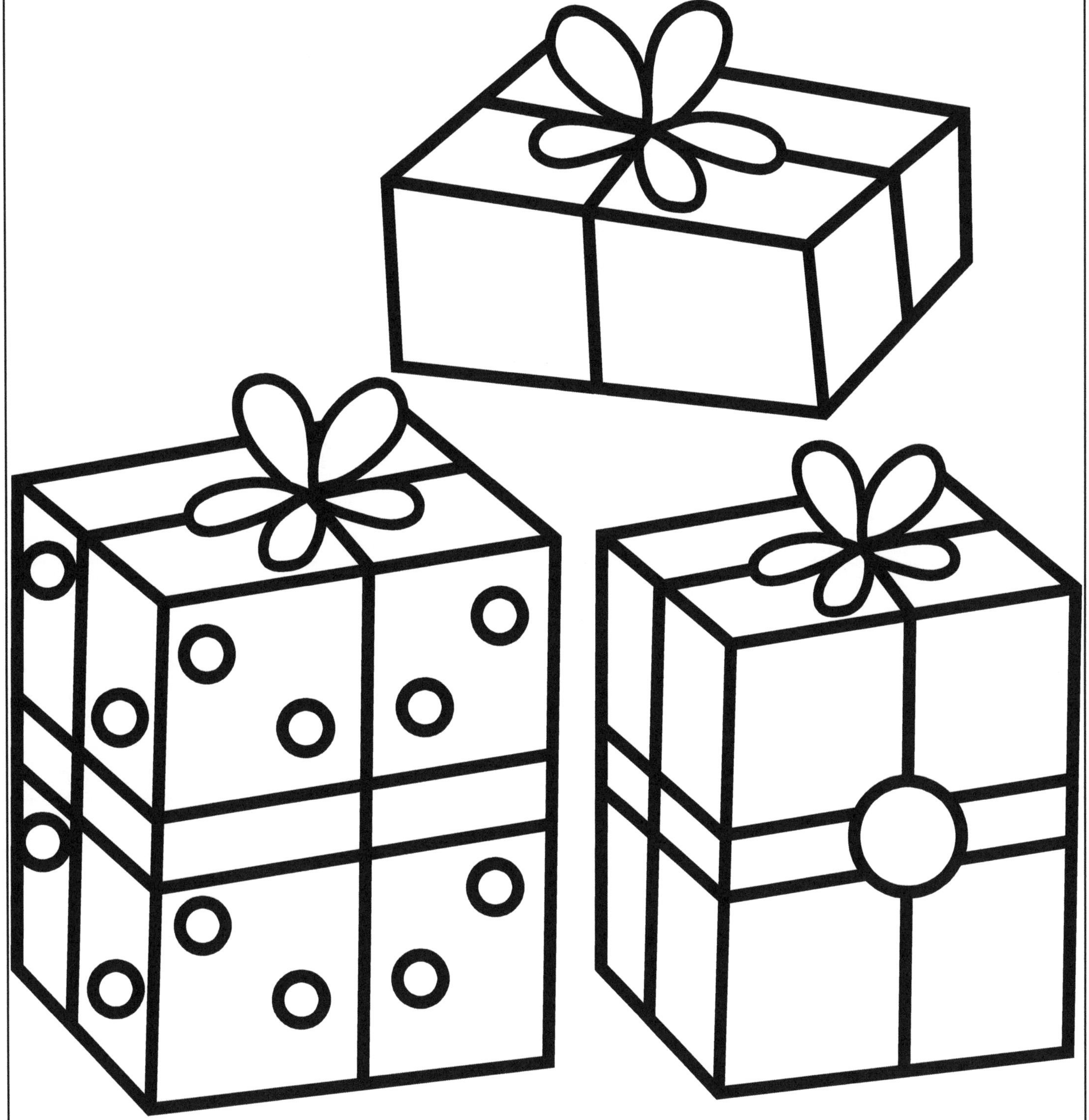

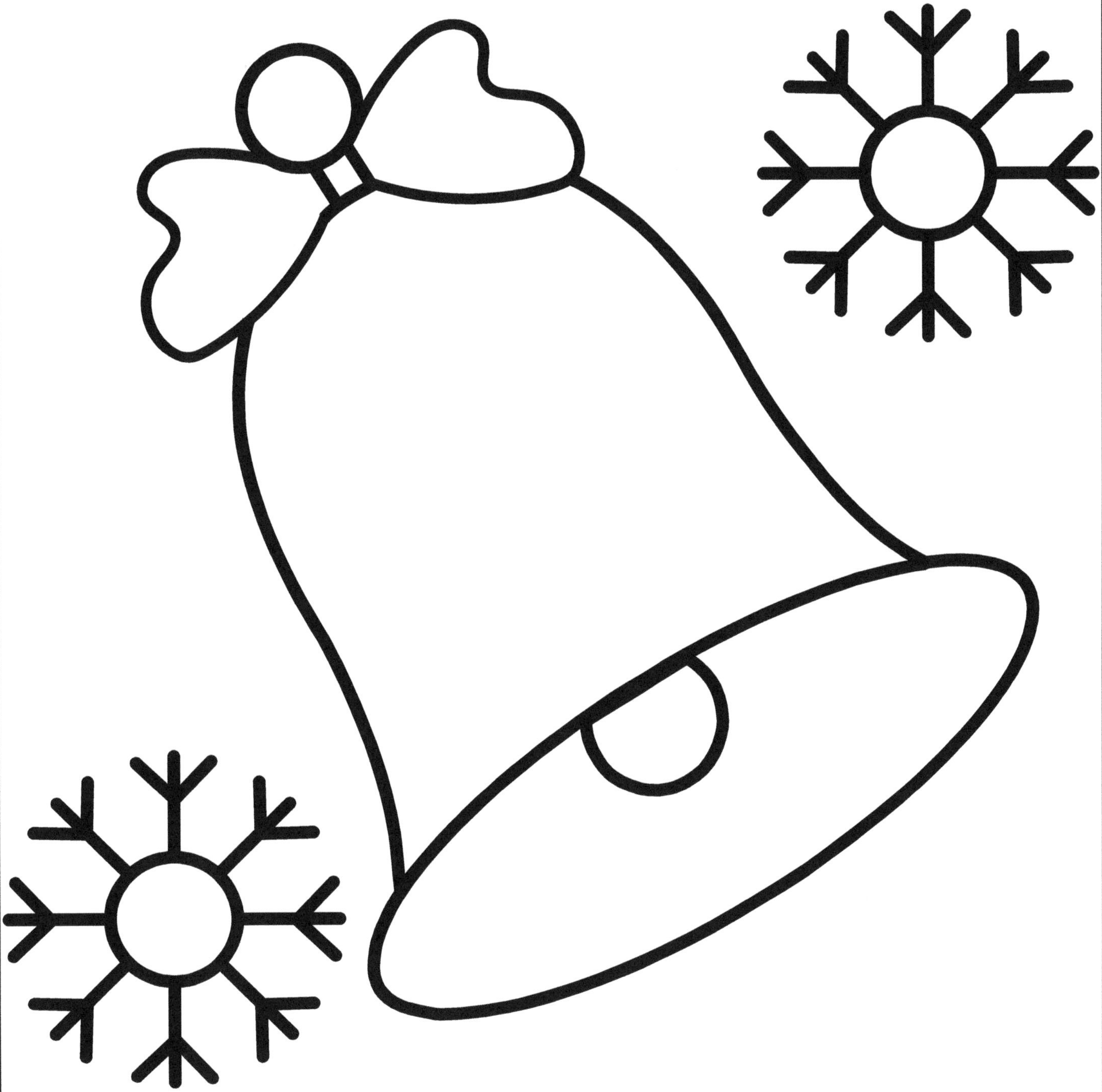

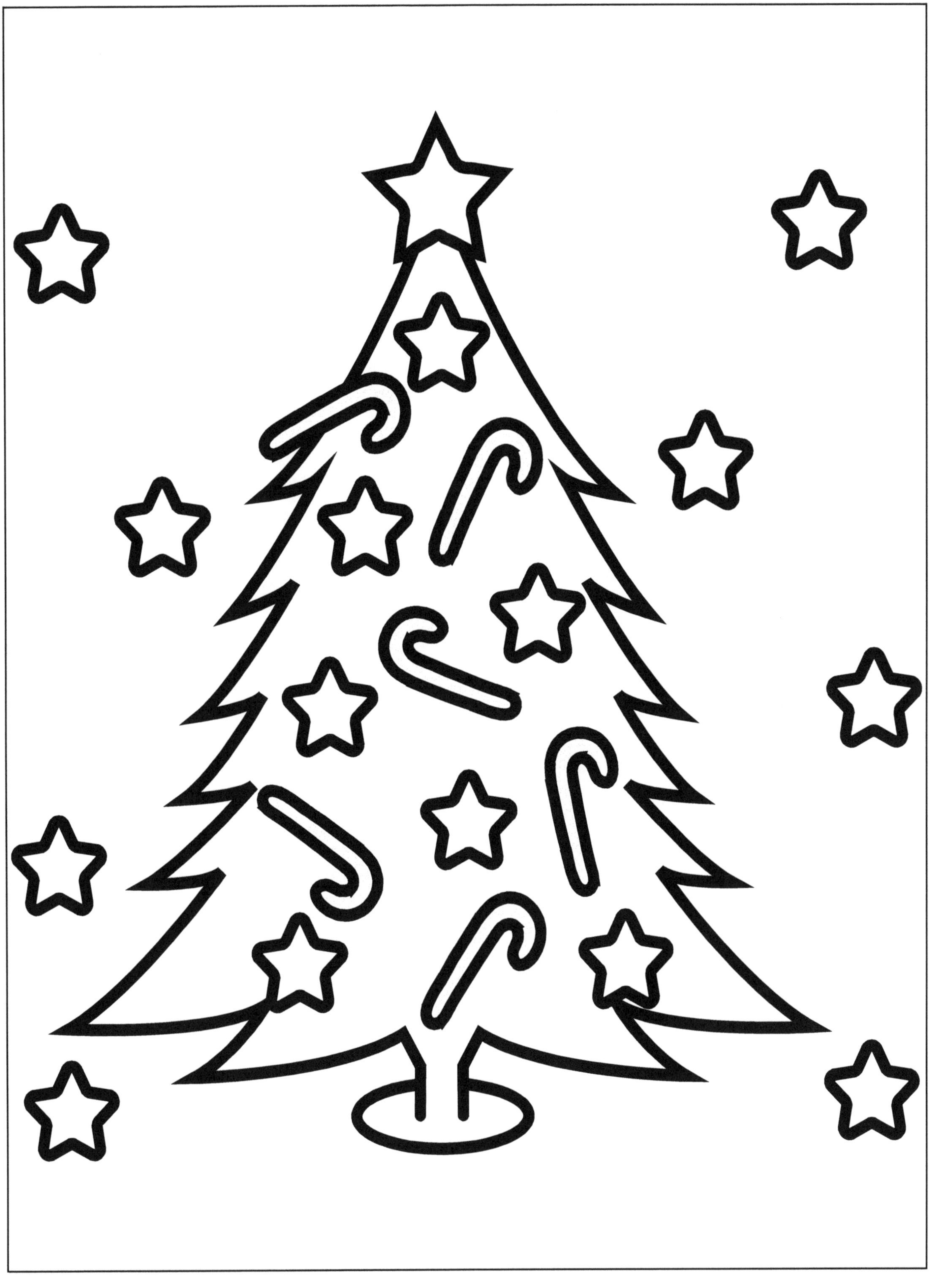

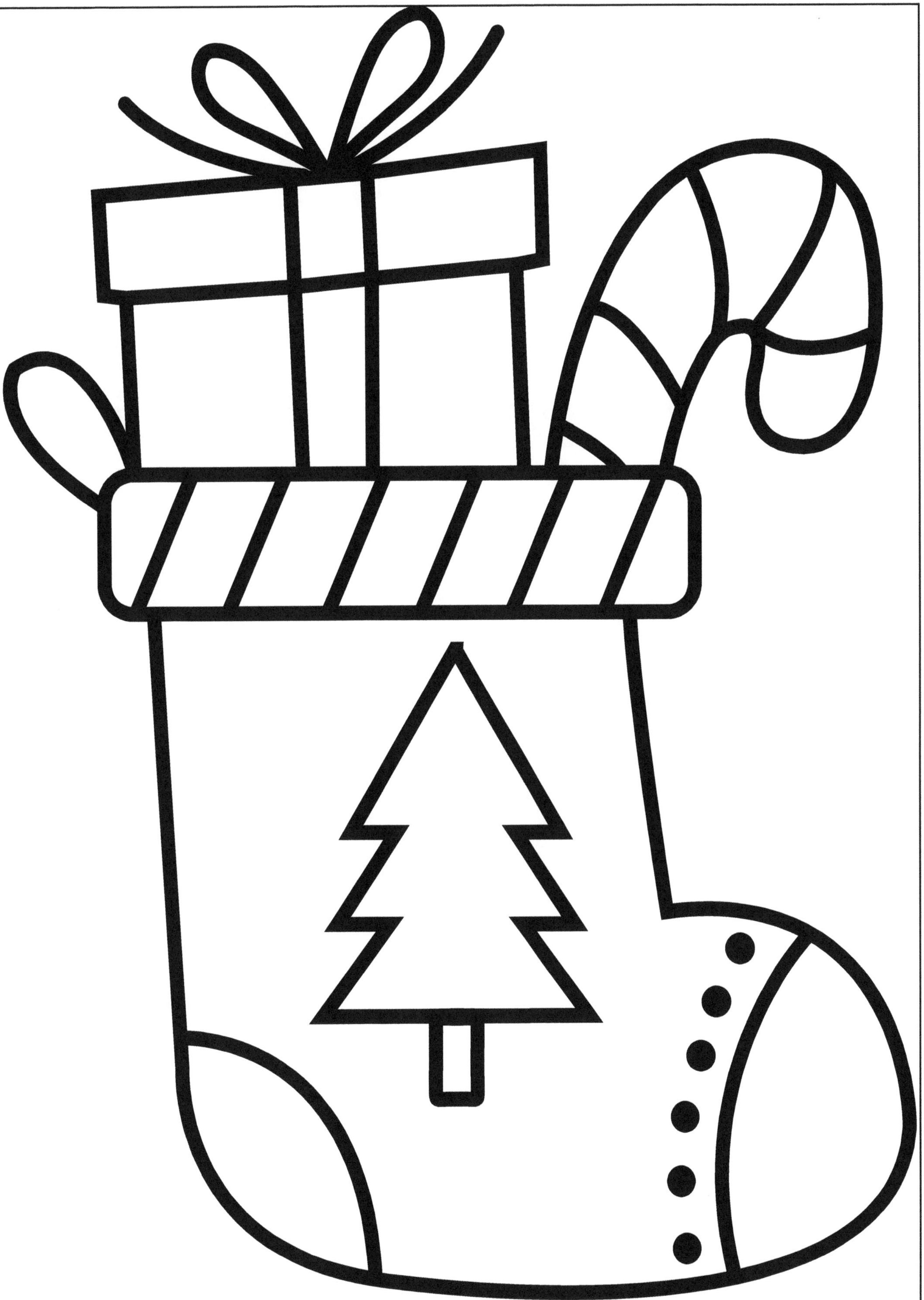

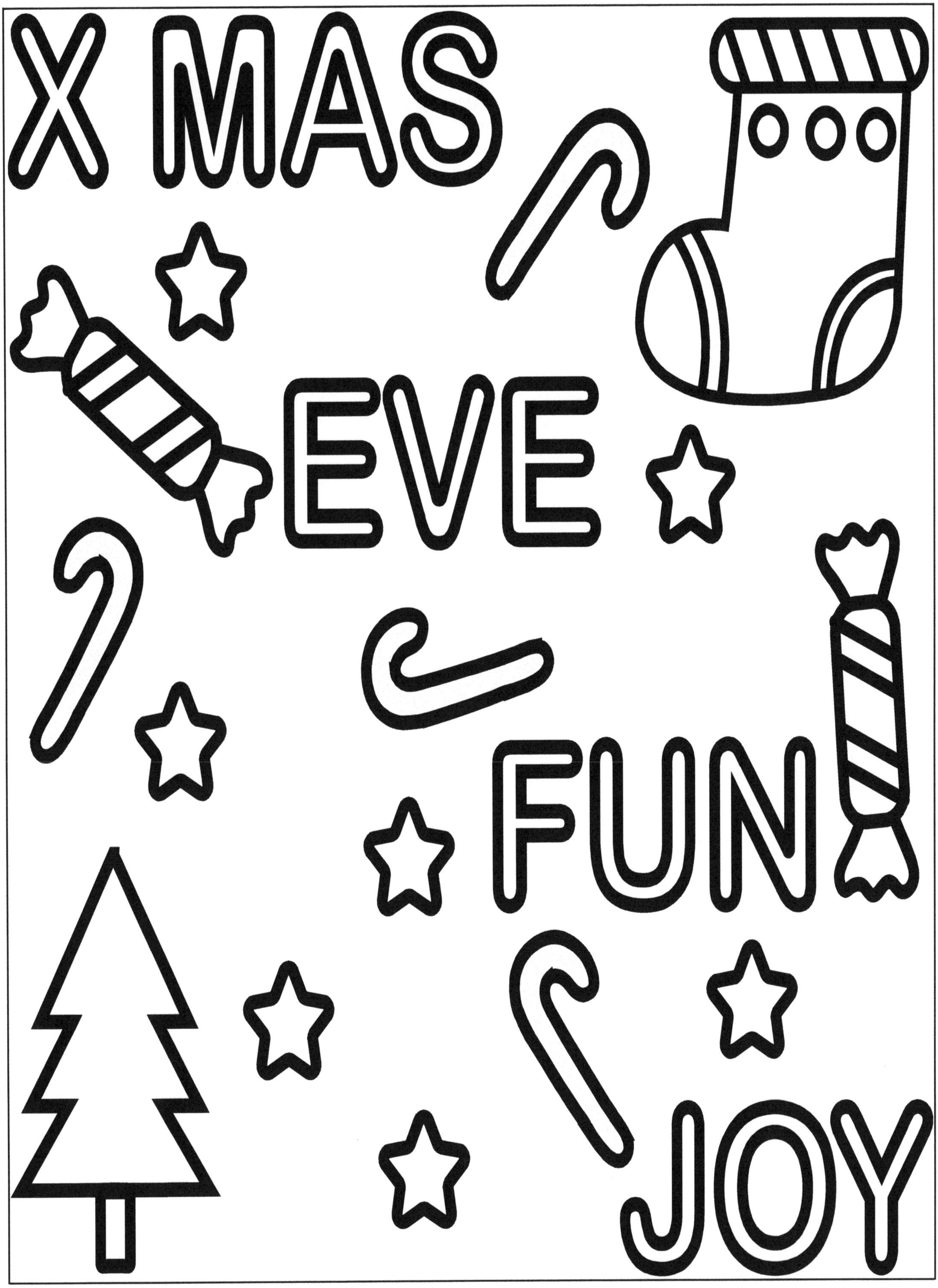
X MAS
EVE
FUN
JOY

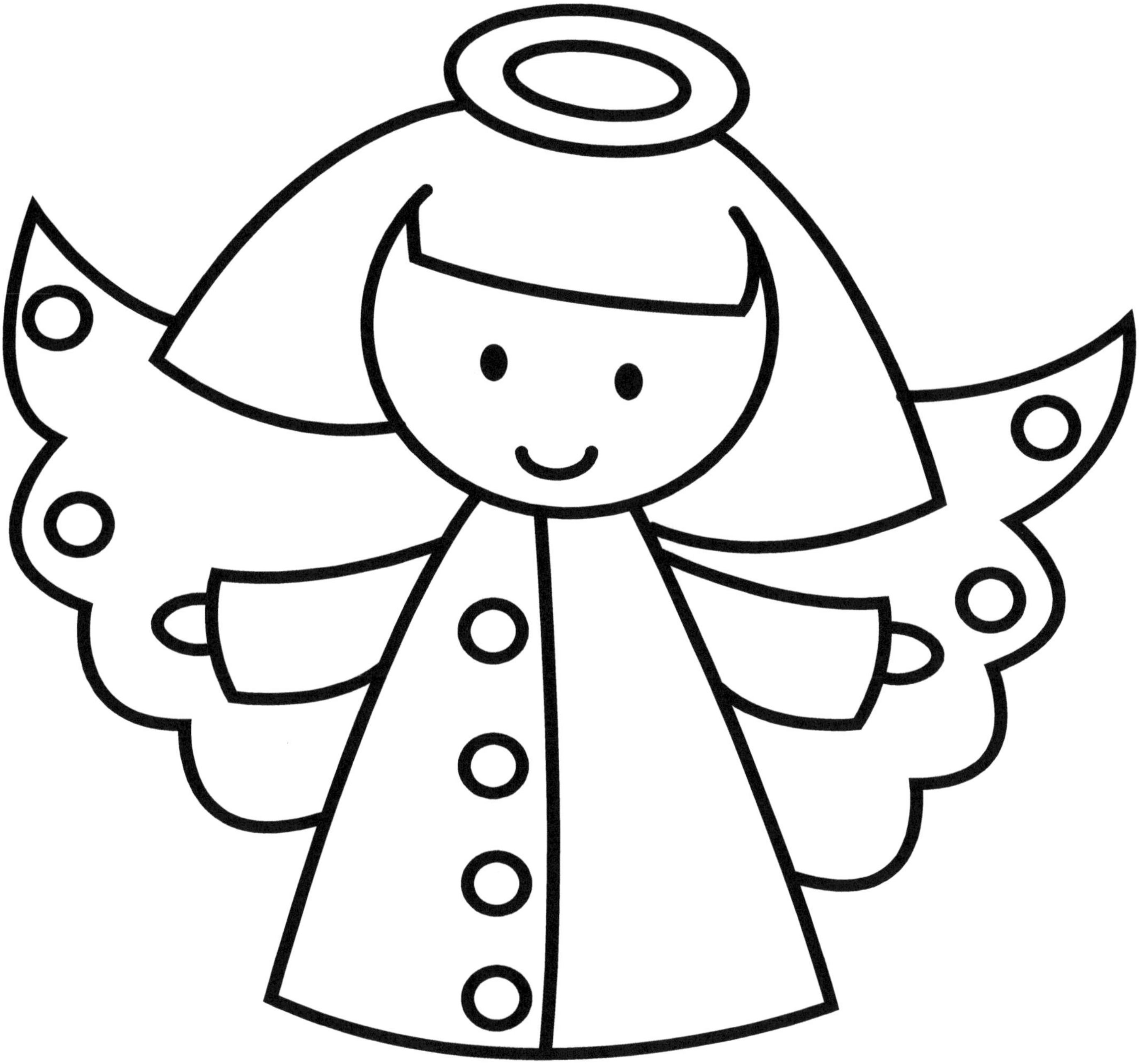

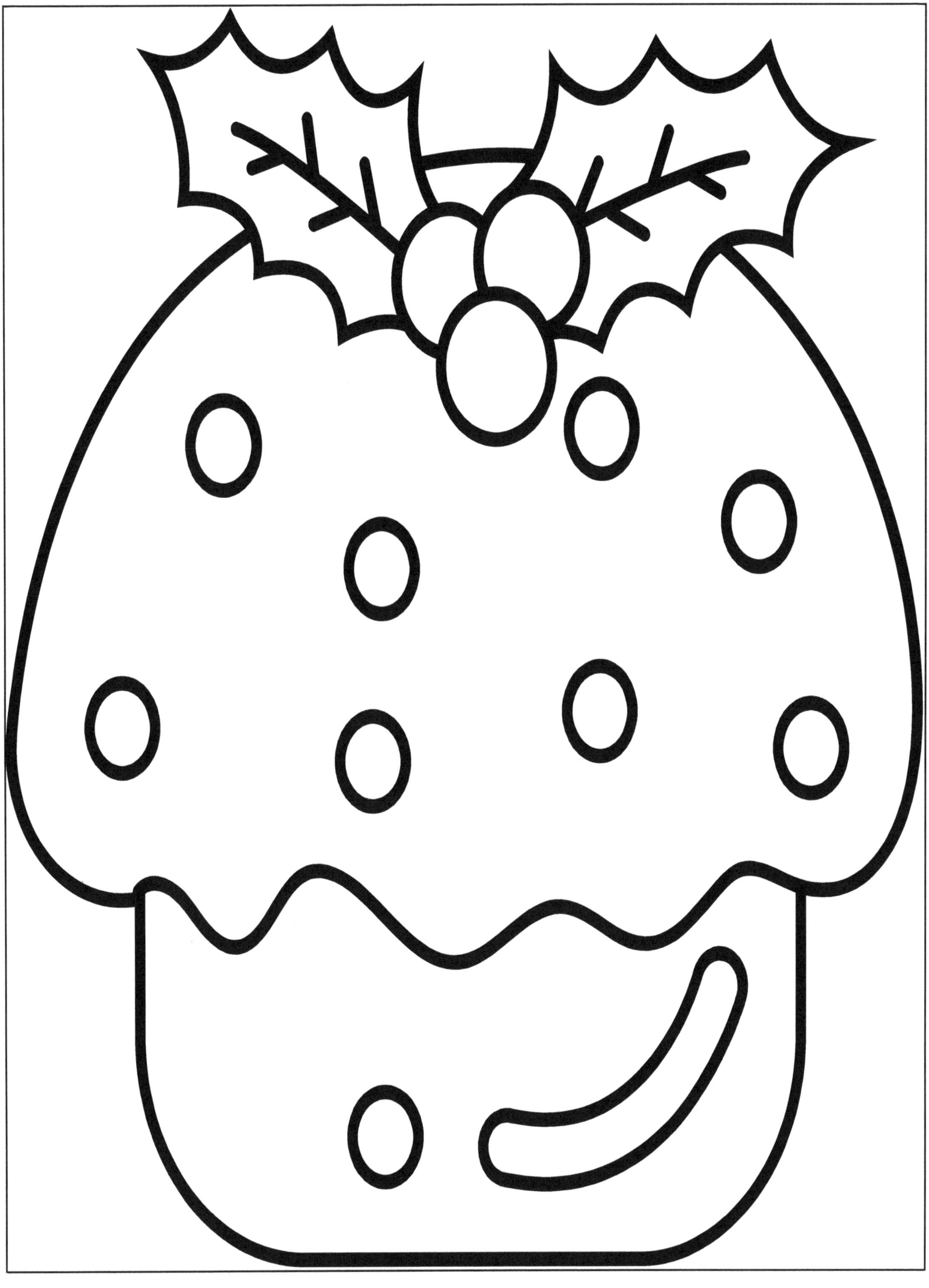

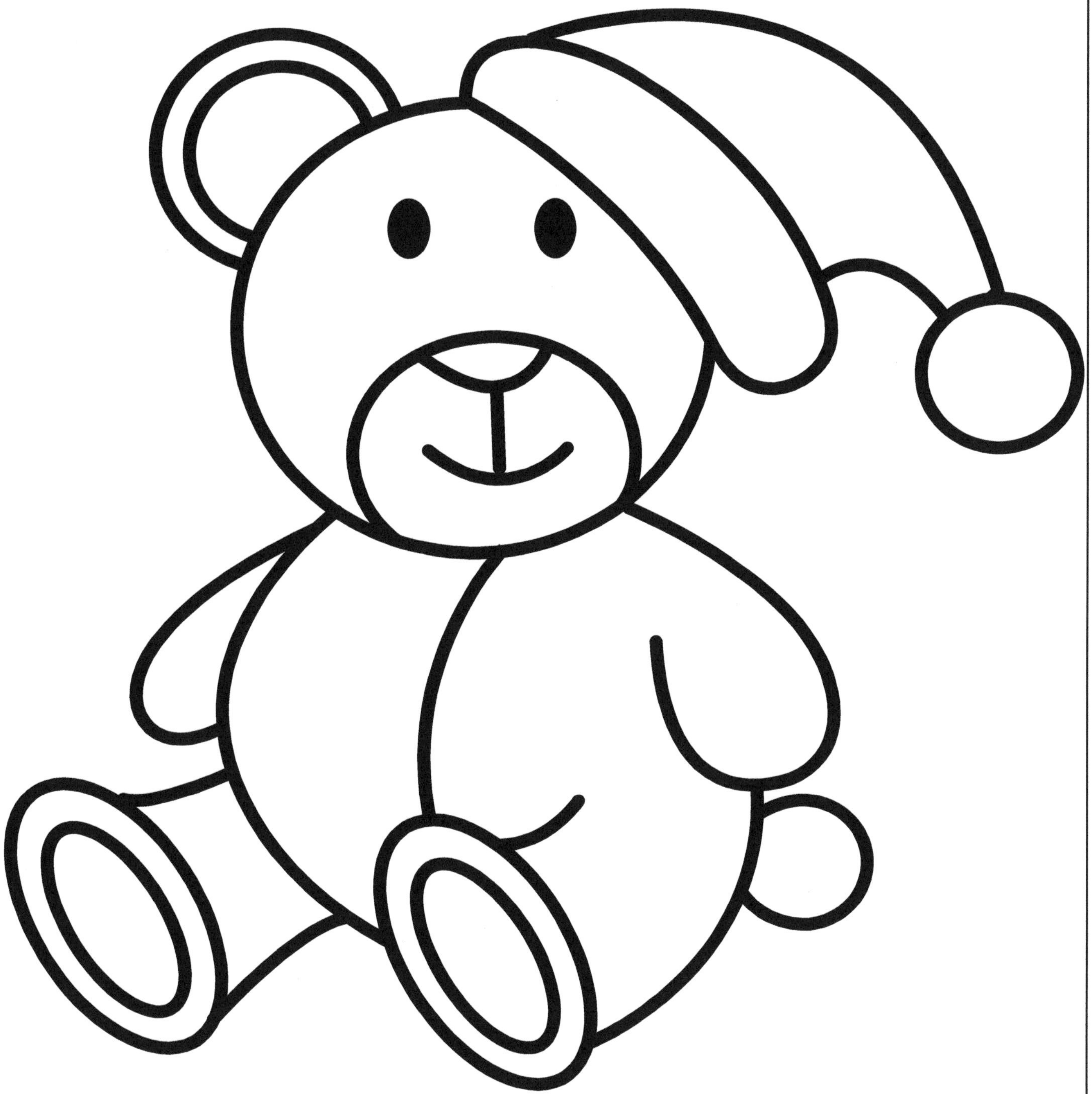

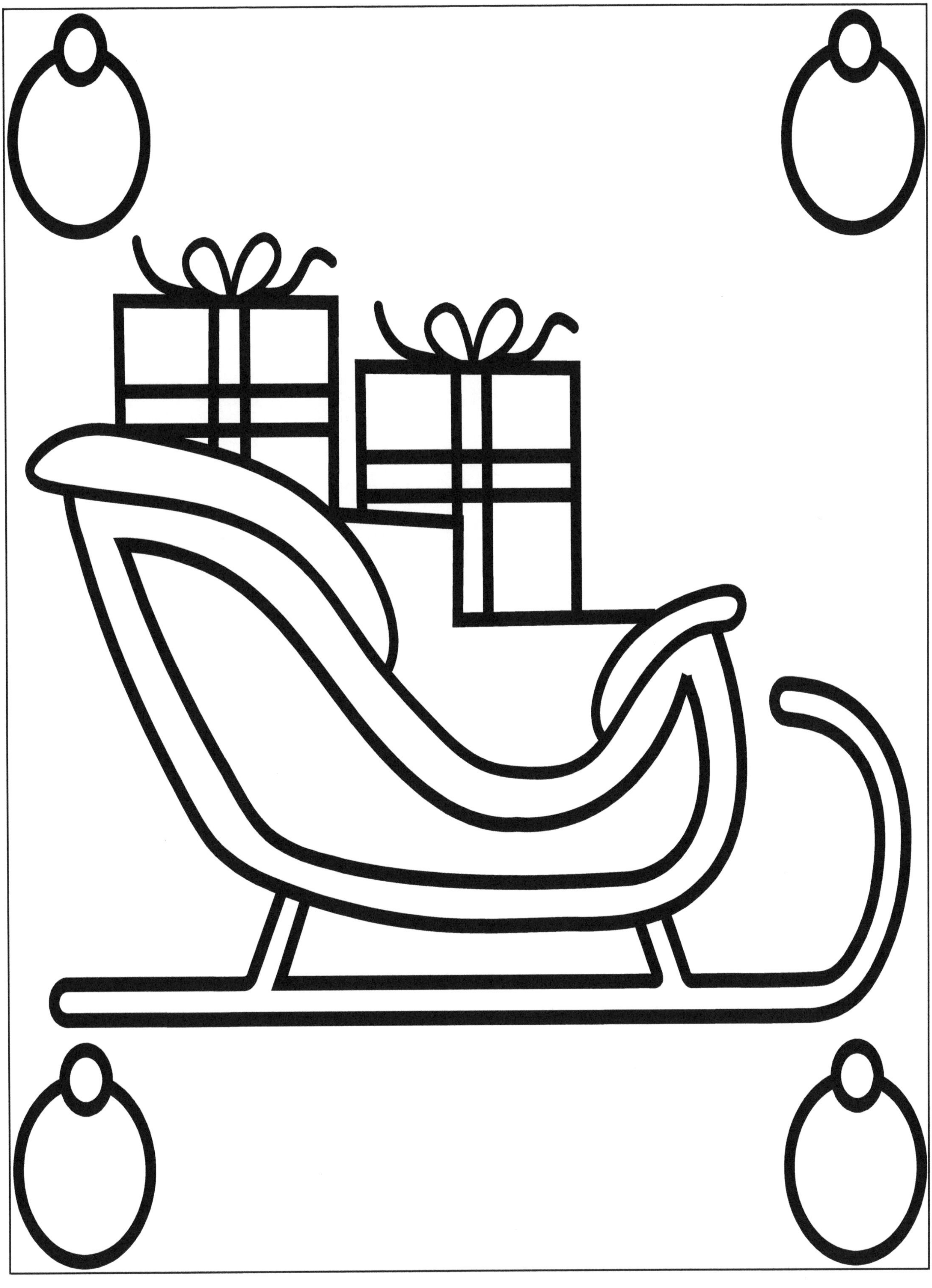

Milton Keynes UK
Ingram Content Group UK Ltd.
UKHW051020270924
448839UK00010B/84